Traditional
Celtic Stories

Lindsay Clarke's
Traditional Celtic Stories

Thorsons

Thorsons
An Imprint of HarperCollins*Publishers*
77–85 Fulham Palace Road,
Hammersmith, London W6 8JB

The Thorsons website address is: www.thorsons.com

First published by Thorsons as *Essential Celtic Mythology* 1997
This edition 1999

1 3 5 7 9 10 8 6 4 2

© Lindsay Clarke

Lindsay Clarke asserts the moral right to
be identified as the author of this work

A catalogue record for this book
is available from the British Library

ISBN 0 7225 3983 5

Printed and bound in Great Britain by
Caledonian Book Manufacturing Ltd, Glasgow

In honour of Donaldeina Cameron (1875–1935)
the grandmother I never met

Contents

Introduction

Asked once to judge between contending poets in Ireland, Colum Cille – who became more widely known as St Columba and was a great prince of the Celtic church – is recorded as saying:

> If poets' verses be but stories
> So be food and raiment stories;
> So is all the world a story;
> So is man of dust a story.

And since all the world is but a story, he asserts, it is better to buy an enduring story rather than one that will not endure.

Columba's insistence on the strangely fictional nature of this world may be characteristically Celtic, but its spirit is echoed many centuries later in what must be among the briefest of all creation myths – the single captivating sentence in which the Jewish writer Elie Wiesel declares that God made people because he loves stories.

Wiesel's is a myth that brings creator and creation so touchingly close that a sceptic might simply reverse its terms and say that people have invented their many gods for much the same reason. After all, as Columba himself suggests, human beings are creatures of story, and a great deal will depend on the kind of stories we choose to tell each other.

As far as we know, the other species live out their lives entirely in the received realm of the natural order, except of course in so far as we have contaminated that order with our own ambitions. We live in that realm too, of course – our lives arise from its processes and we remain finally dependent on them for our sustenance – but things are more complicated for us because we also live inside a world of stories. What I like about both the terms of Columba's judgment and the implication of Elie Wiesel's myth is their recognition that the capacity to tell stories lies close to the very essence of what makes us human.

It may be unsurprising that a novelist should feel that way; storytellers have a vested interest in such matters after all. But isn't storytelling what we all do, most of the time? We tell our lives in stories – the story of our day, of our journey, of our accidents and adventures, our joys and griefs and tribulations. It's how we make sense of ourselves and what happens to us. It's how we shape raw events into communicable experience and open passages from feeling into meaning. It's how we imagine our personal world into being.

Although in recent years the commercialization of the world has put a premium on information, we don't share our important experiences by trading information: we do it by telling stories. And if stories are the currency through which we exchange our intimate personal humanity, they also underpin our thinking about the public world.

It's worth recalling here that the word *world* derives from the Anglo-Saxon roots *wer*, meaning *man*, and *eld* which means *age*; so etymologically it signifies an age of man. Or, to expand it a little, a version of reality that holds good among men for a time. A man-age-ment system, if you like.

The existence of such a world is sanctioned by a story, or collection of stories which, as long as it remains vital in the imagination of its hearers, will be experienced not merely as fictional but as the very fabric of reality itself. We call such stories myths and, properly understood, myths are world-endowed stories – stories by which communities of people live, and for which they are often prepared both to die and to kill. For such stories are so numinous with meaning that they can be seen as fictional only by those who do not inhabit the reality they sanction. (And also, I should probably add, by those within that world who have come to understand that all such stories point beyond their images to a deeper reality that cannot otherwise be articulated – that they are what Joseph Campbell memorably called his history of mythology the *Masks of God*).

A cultural world will thrive as long as it retains confidence in its stories. When those stories prove unreliable, when they cease to correspond with lived experience and no longer seem to work (as sooner or later happens to all of them because the universe seems to expand in response to our attempts to explain it), then that world is in trouble. For this reason imperialists have long recognized that you will reduce a conquered people to subjection more quickly if you demean the dignity of their language and demoralize belief in the validity of their myths.

Once this is understood we begin to see why, for so long, there has been so little general familiarity with the Celtic gods and goddesses that were once native to the hills and groves of the British Isles —except, of course, in those regions where the cultural identity of the Welsh, Irish and Scottish peoples has been faithfully preserved.

Two thousand years ago each of our springs, rivers, forests, tors and coombes would have been consecrated to one or other of the Celtic deities. The stories associated with them would have been an indelible part of tribal memory, told and retold down the generations in every settlement. But since the Emperor Claudius declared the Celtic realms of southern Britain a Roman province, these islands have been invaded many times, and just as the Celts themselves once displaced indigenous cultures in their own expansion across Europe, so the Romans, Angles, Saxons, Jutes and Norsemen later overlaid their own powerful stories on Celtic traditions.

Out of that rich mix eventually emerged the dominant culture of a southern English aristocracy whose classical education was largely founded on the rites of Christianity and the myths of Greece and Rome. Small wonder then that, in a culture where rational scepticism has since subsequently diminished the very word 'myth' to mean only that which is demonstrably false and untrue, the names and nature of our native Celtic gods are known to hardly anyone but a few scholars and enthusiasts.

Like the gods themselves, however, good stories never die, and those who know and love what remains to us of the ancient Celtic myths have an increasingly confident sense that our delight in them, far from being merely academic or antiquarian, may turn out to be a significant expression – one among many – of a newly vigorous, vital mode of consciousness.

I'll have more to say about that in a moment, but first we should take a look at who the people were who originally told these marvellous stories, and give some thought to the modifying, even disfiguring, means by which their myths have endured across the centuries.

To the Greeks the Celts were known as *Keltoi* or, in a variant form, *Galatae*. The Romans, who respected and at times had cause to fear them as one of the four great peoples surrounding their mediterranean world, called them *Celtae* or *Galli*, and the fact that the language of the Western Isles is still known as Gaelic while, far to the east of what was once called Gaul, a province of Asia Minor was still recently referred to as Galatia, gives some idea of the influence and power once wielded by their culture.

The Celts enter recorded history in the sixth century BCE. By the end of the third century their restless expansive energy had conquered and settled almost the whole of central Europe and many of its southern regions, from Spain through northern Italy into the Balkans and areas of Greece and Turkey. But the Celts met powerful competition for these vast tracts of land from the Germanic and Dacian tribes, as well as from the rising power across the Alps in Rome; and though they were passionately fierce fighters – a head-hunting, aristocratic warrior-culture, whose women were feared in battle as much as their men – they lacked both the talent and the taste for a highly centralized system of military and political organization, such as would prove to be the directing strength of the Roman Empire. By the time Julius Caesar marched his legions against Gagul the scope of Celtic influence had already declined elsewhere in Europe, and when Gaul was defeated, Britain became for a while the principal centre of resistance to Roman expansion in the west.

Various Celtic tribes had settled these islands in successive waves of immigration over the previous centuries. These were the 'Ancient Britons' abou;t whom we were taught in Junior School.

Under leaders such as Caratacus and Boudicca some of those tribes mounted ferocious resistance to Roman imperial ambitions, although others were content to become prosperous client states. After the genocidal defeat of the Iceni by Suetonius Paulinus, however, it was only a question of time before all but the peoples of Scotland, Ireland and the wilder reaches of Wales were absorbed into the Roman Imperium. When the last resistance was subdued by Agricola, all of Britain south of Caledonia was colonized, and a distinctively Romano-British culture with its own pagan and, later, Christian rites, swiftly evolved. This culture would play a significant role in maintaining the empire's authority during some of its darkest days. In the years of its final decline, one of the greatest of Celtic mythic heroes, Arthur himself, may well have become conflated with the historical figure of a Romano-Celtic Dux Bellorum, whose highly mobile cavalry-command successfully defended the island for a time against invading English foes. Ironically, it is through that tradition (and the uses made of it by the Angevins and, much later, the Victorians) that Celtic mythology has most vividly exercised its influence on English literature.

Classical writers distinguished Celtic culture from others of the ancient world by the nature of their religious beliefs, their characteristic mode of dress, manner of fighting and system of social organization; but modern scholars regard the variant dialects of their unwritten language as the single most defining feature of the Celtic tribes. Apart from surviving inscriptions, the Gaulish language has vanished altogether now, but the Goidelic dialect can still be heard in Irish, Manx and Scottish Gaelic, while the

Brythonic form, once spoken by the Bretons and the Cornish, still thrives in Wales. But whatever dialect they spoke, the Celts were famous in the ancient world for the compelling power of their eloquence.

Diodorus Siculus remarked on the rich figurative power and the witty riddling allusiveness of their speech, along with what he considered to be a weakness for boasting and grandiloquent exaggeration. The high regard in which the Celts held such virtuosity with language is vividly illustrated by their reverence for the god Ogmios. The Greek writer Lucian tells us how, while travelling in Gaul, he came upon an image of an old man clad in a lion's skin who was leading an enchanted group of followers. They were drawn along behind him willingly and irresistibly because their ears were fastened to his tongue by delicate chains forged of amber and gold. This was Ogmios. Likening the figure to that of Heracles, Lucian's Gaulish guide remarked that the Celts believed eloquence to be far more powerful than mere brute strength, and not least because its fluency increases rather than declines with age.

The language of the Celts remained without a written form till the fifth century of the Christian Era, so they assigned immense value both to powers of memory and to the imaginative impact of the spoken word. Their myths, religious beliefs, ritual and oracular practices, hymns and praise-songs, poems, craft-mysteries, histories, genealogies, laws, lore, in fact all the interrelated spiritual and intellectual resources of their culture, were entirely preserved through an oral tradition that was carefully guarded and propagated by the various orders of druids, bards and ovates. Among their other roles, these figures were the living memory-bank of the tribe, and their hugely influential status could be achieved only through rigorous years of initiatory training.

It is to those powerful arts of memory and eloquence that we ulti-
mately owe the survival of the Celtic Myths; but only a part of what
must have once been their staggering riches has come down to us,
and sadly, as far as the Welsh stories are concerned, in much contaminated form.

Times change and stories change with them. Over long centuries of conflict, aboriginally matriarchal cultures were displaced
by aristocratic male-dominated warrior societies, which were
themselves later qualified and reinterpreted by a new, exclusive
religion often fiercely intolerant of the old. Even the locally Celtic
character of Christianity would eventually be modified by rules
imposed from Rome. So to go to the medieval texts which are our
surviving records of the Celtic myths is a little like visiting a rich
archaeological site in which only relics remain of what once must
have been a mythic universe as lively, subtle, delicate and coher-
ent as the more completely preserved mythologies of the classical
world.

Writing of the *Mabinogion* in his *Study of Celtic Literature*, Matthew
Arnold remarks that the first thing that strikes one is 'how evidently the medieval storyteller is pillaging an antiquity of which he
does not fully possess the secret: he is like a peasant building his
hut on the side of Halicarnassus or Ephesus; he builds, but what
he builds is full of materials of which he knows not the history, or
knows by a glimmering tradition merely: stones "not of this
building", but of an older architecture, greater, cunninger, more
majestic … they belong to an older, pagan, mythological world.'

Even the more finely preserved Irish stories were depleted of
religious significance by the time they came to be written down.

One scribe, writing in *The Book of the Dun Cow* around 1100, concedes that though the learned men did not know where the Tuatha de Danann came from, 'it seems likely to them that they came from heaven on account of their intelligence and for the excellence of their knowledge.' Another thought it necessary to point out that although he was enumerating the Celtic gods, he did not worship them; and we can still hear the uneasy scepticism with which a third monk regarded the manuscript of the *Tain Bo Cuailnge* (*The Cattle Raid of Cooley*), for which he was responsible. 'I who have written out this history, or more properly fiction,' he adds in a colophon, 'do not accept as matter of belief certain things in this history, or rather fiction; for some things are diabolical impositions, some are poetical inventions, some have a semblance of truth, some have not, and some are meant to be the entertainment of fools.'

So, as their nature and deeds passed through the filter of such monkish sensibilities, the awesome gods of the Celts were diminished into heroic human figures possessed of magical powers. Even more drastically, their goddesses such as Danu and Macha, who were evidently once supreme in the imagination of the people, are reduced in the surviving texts to little more than powerfully emotive names. The exception is the Morrigan, the furious she-crow of battle whose terrible shadow lies across so many of the ancient Irish tales.

Nevertheless, though no Celtic creation myth survives, some of the principal deities in the Celtic pantheon can be seen wielding their powers in the first of the stories, *The Coming of Lugh*. The story tells how Ireland was settled by successive waves of immigration until the Tuatha de Danann, the people of the Goddess Danu (who correspond to the Children of Don in Welsh stories) made the land their own by defeating their monstrous rivals, the Firbolgs and the Fomors.

Danu herself is referred to as the Mother of the Gods, but in the version of the myth that has come down to us the focus remains firmly on her male progeny. Prominent among these is the Dagda ('The Good God' – good in the sense of 'skillful' or 'excelling') who is sometimes called 'the father-of-all', and who sired the wily love-god, Aengus, and Brigid who presided over the arts of poetry and learning. At the time of the first battle with the Firbolgs, Nuada was king and war-leader of the *Tuatha de Danann*. Known as *Argetlam* because of the silver hand that was fashioned to replace the one he lost in battle, Nuada corresponds to the Welsh Nudd or Nodens, in whose name a dream-temple was consecrated at Lydney on the banks of the Severn in Gloucestershire. It was Goibniu, smith among the gods, who fashioned that wonderful hand, while Diancecht was physician to the gods. Ogma was a variant of the Gaulish Ogmios in both physical strength and skill with language, and Lugh himself was admitted to the company of the gods not for one specific skill but because he was master of all the arts. Though we know little of the sea-god Lir, the magical powers of his son Manannan often play a key role in both Irish and Welsh stories, where he is known as Manawyddan.

Other Celtic deities feature in the following stories but there are many that we know of who do not, and those readers who wish to know more about the gods and religion of the Celtic peoples – of 'ruthless Teutates, Esus whose savage shrine makes men shudder, and Taranis whose altar is no more benign than that of Scythian Diana,' (as Lucian described them twenty centuries ago); or of the horned god Cernunnos and the horse-goddess Epona whose emblems may be carved in chalk across the downland scarps of England; or of the relation these and other misty deities might have to the mysterious cults of heads, and animals, and wells ... – such readers are advised to consult the fine scholarly works of Anne Ross, Myles Dillon, Nora Chadwick, Stuart Pigott and others in the recently energized realm of Celtic studies. For this is not a book about Celtic Mythology, but a contemporary retelling of some ancient Celtic myths, and its intention is simply to offer the general reader a lively, accessible version of stories that deserve to be more widely known and loved by the English-speaking peoples.

Apart from *The Coming of Lugh* which is taken from a text generally known as *The Book of Ivasions*, the Irish stories here are derived from the Ulster Cycle and the Fenian Cycle. The Ulster Cycle may have been written down as early as the seventh century but is far more ancient than that in its celebration of heroic values kindred to those of the Iliad. *The Sorrows of Deirdre* is a fore-tale of the Ulster Cycle and *The Cattle-Raid of Cuailnge*, its central theme, is one that was dearly prized down the generations by the bards. Another Ulster tale, that of *The Shoes of the Leprechaun* has been added both for the leaven of humour it brings to the mix and for its illustration of the way mythology shades off into folklore. The Fenian Cycle did not achieve comprehensive form till the twelfth century text known as *The Colloquy of the Ancients* in which Cailte recounts the adventures of Finn's fighting men – the *fiana* – to St Patrick. Its feel is more humane, less archetypically heroic than that of the Ulster Cycle, and *The Pursuit of Diarmaid and Grainne* is one of the most moving stories from that cycle of tales.

The four Welsh stories are each taken from one of the four branches of the *Mabinogion* – that medieval treasure-house of story in which archaic mythic tropes are so caparisoned with all the heraldic trappings of feudal romance that I felt it necessary to stay loyal in the retelling to that later evolution of the Celtic imagination.

The four Welsh stories are each taken from one of the four branches of the *Mabinogion* – that medieval treasure-house of story in which archaic mythic tropes are so caparisoned with all the heraldic trappings of feudal romance that I felt it necessary to stay loyal in the retelling to that later evolution of the Celtic imagination.

These, then, are not translations of the ancient texts but new English versions of the stories they record – versions which try to stay faithful both to the spirit and to the substance of the stories as we have inherited them, while at the same time making them more accessible to a general readership than translations have sometimes proved to be. For that reason I have tended to prefer those spellings of the names of people and places which seemed least likely to deter English readers (Conor rather than Conchobar, for example), and have tried to find a style which echoes some of the cadences of Celtic speech without drifting into pastiche. The hope was that they would lift easily off the page to the eye while also sounding well when read aloud.

There are, of course, real difficulties with such an enterprise, and if the language seems not Celtic enough in feel to some readers, or too 'high' to others whose taste is for a plain, contemporary manner, then I offer in plea of mitigation to the former the desire to hold an English audience, and would remind the latter that these are not only archetypal tales of gods and heroic figures, but the mythic tradition of a people who revered high speech.

This feels like a good moment to be retelling these ancient Celtic stories. We are living through transitional times which have called into question many orthodoxies and conventions that not so long ago felt reasonably secure. New perspectives arising from relativity theory in physics, from the findings of the depth psychologists, from anthropological and ecological studies, from our post-imperial, perhaps even post-industrial situation, and the consequent deconstruction of the largely masculine tradition of western thought – these and other related developments have all stimulated a new interrogative awareness of 'reality' as a mytholigical function of the human imagination. In such uneasy times we feel our own once reliable stories wearing perilously thin, but new stories commanding general assent have not yet emerged.

Perhaps for this reason – and out of an increasingly anxious conviction that the intellectual mainstream of the west may have brought us to an imminently disastrous pass – there is a greater interest now than at any other time in what has long been derided, oppressed and unrecognized in the wisdom traditions of cultures other than our own.

Though it has been present in these islands almost long enough to be considered aboriginal, Celtic culture remains for most English people an exotic tradition, one that has been marginalized both geographically and culturally for centuries. Yet it may be that as western consciousness seeks to evolve beyond the limitations of Newtonian and Cartesian conventions of thought, the particular qualities of the Celtic vision have a compensatory value for our time. Read in that context, it seems to me that these ancient myths are filled with hints about things we urgently need to know.

In their fluent trafficking between this world and the other-world, for example, they vividly illustrate relations between the conscious and the unconscious realms of our experience, and might thereby help us to assimilate the radical insights of the depth psychologists. Similarly their vision of the shape-shifting immateriality of the visible world feels consistent with the quantum physicists' picture of the fugitive nature of matter, while at the same time it reinforces the contemporary 'postmodern' insight that 'reality' is a fictional construct, endlessly porous to the imagination, and therefore susceptible to imaginative change.

We sense too that, even though it has been heavily overlaid by the warrior-values of a patriarchal order, there lies at the deepest levels of these stories a respect for the archetypal power of the female principle, and an understanding that its claims must be honoured in and by people of both genders if life is to be lived whole. Beyond that, in their celebration of the awesome, often destructive power of human passions, these stories compel us to recognize how complex and dangerous human beings truly are – that nothing in our nature can safely be left out of consideration, and that what is repressed and denied will not just go harmlessly away but will come back seeking expression – sometimes vengefully, and therefore at painful cost both to others and ourselves.

For there is nothing evasive or sentimental in these myths. Indeed they are often ferocious, violent and bloody, and precisely because of that they may serve to remind us that the crying need of our own time is for stories that seek out values larger than merely tribal loyalties; and that failure to find such new, more widely embracing myths will condemn our children to the grievous deadlocked battles of the past.

But these old stories are enlarging and poetic too. As well as violence and tragedy and death there is reconciliation and renewal here. Above all they seem to rejoice in the inventive power of the imagination, both human and divine, and the hope is that, in making them available once more, they will touch and stimulate the imagination of the reader as powerfully as they have moved and nourished mine.

PART ONE

IRISH MYTHS

1

The Coming of Lugh

Long before the Gaels arrived in Ireland, that green place had been the country of the *Tuatha de Danann*, the people of the earth-goddess Danu, who were themselves honoured as gods by the Gaels. Some say that Danu's people came out of the north, others that they were from the southern islands of the world, and there is an older story still that they descended to Ireland through the high air of the sky.

What is certain is that the People of Danu had previously lived in four great cities – Findias, Gorias, Murias and Falias – where they had grown skilled in the arts of poetry and magic. For that reason they were able to come ashore on the island under the protection of a powerful enchantment. And so it was that at the feast of Beltane on the first of May they arrived in Ireland in the shape of a shining mist of dense cloud.

When they came to Ireland they carried with them a treasure of great power from each of their four cities. A sword whose stroke none might escape was brought out of the city of Findias. From

Gorias was brought a terrible lance that could be kept at rest only by steeping its head in a brew of poppy leaves. Out of Murias came the great cauldron from which none went away unthankful; and from the city of Falias was fetched that stone, the *Lia Fail* – the Stone of Destiny – which would cry out with a human cry whenever the rightful king of Ireland should lay his hand upon it.

Now the people of Danu were not themselves the first to come to Ireland. In the remote time when the whole island was no more than a single treeless plain with only three lakes watered by no more than nine rivers, the race of Partholon had come there out of the Otherworld. As those early settlers increased, the island enlarged itself under their rule, but they had to fight for their expanding land.

For a time savage wars were fought with the Fomors – a race of deformed giants who rose from the dark deeps of the sea. At last victory was won and thereafter Partholon's people enjoyed peace for three hundred prosperous years until, within the space of a single week, they were destroyed by a terrible plague, and withdrew again into the Otherworld.

The island increased its size still further under the rule of the next people to come there, the race of a king called Nemed. These newcomers were also greatly oppressed by the dark power of the

Fomors, to whom they were forced to pay tribute of two-thirds of each year's harvest, together with two-thirds of all the children born to them.

After Nemed died from an infectious sickness, his people fought a disastrous campaign against the Fomorian stronghold in the glass tower on Tory Island. Though the tower was taken, only thirty of Nemed's people were left alive out of the sixteen thousand who went to fight in that terrible war of weapons and dark enchantments. So Ireland stood open once more.

When the People of Danu arrived there in the magic mist they were ruled by their king Nuada and his proud queen Macha, who fought in battle as fiercely as her lord. Greatest among their many leaders was the Dagda – 'the Good God' – guardian of the great cauldron of plenty that was brought to Ireland out of Murias. His son Aengus was the protector of lovers, and it is said that his kisses became birds that hovered over the heads of the people of Ireland filling them with thoughts of love. The mightiest of champions among these people was Ogma, whose prodigious strength was matched only by his love for poetry and eloquence; and the relentless force of their fighting power was assured by the Morrigan, the terrible she-crow of battle.

Yet the People of Danu were not only warriors. They also had among their number masters of all the peaceful arts.

At the time of their arrival Ireland was controlled by the Fomorians to the north, and ruled in the south by a dark people called the Firbolg, who had come there earlier out of Greece or Spain. For a time the Firbolg and the People of Danu negotiated with each other cautiously, admiring the different fashioning of each other's weapons while each assessed the strength of the other side. But the king of the Firbolg was called Eochaid the Proud, and when the People of Danu suggested that it would be wisest to divide the island peacefully between their two races, it was he who said, 'If once we give these people half the land, soon enough they will take the whole.'

So the peaceable terms offered by the Tuatha de Danann were refused and the armies of the two peoples met in battle on Midsummer Day across a plain in Connaught. It was a fight that lasted for four hot brutal days.

In that savage conflict Nuada, king of the People of Danu, saw his hand shorn off by a Firbolg champion, together with half his shield. Yet the battle gradually began to turn his way when Eochaid, the Firbolg king, who was sweating in the heat of his armour and suffering from thirst, led off a hundred of his warriors to search for water. His company travelled as far as Sligo where the horsemen of Danu caught up with him and cut him down.

His people fought on until only three hundred of them were left alive, and even then the remaining Firbolg warriors dared their enemies to duel in single combat until all of them were dead. Impressed by their dogged valour, Nuada would not hear of this. Instead he generously offered the remnant of the Firbolg race a fifth part of the island to keep for ever as their own; and so the People of Danu came to rule over all the former lands of the Firbolg excepting Connaught itself.

After the battle, the physician Diancecht used all his skill to replace the king's lost hand with an artificial one he had made from silver. The metal was so cunningly wrought that it could freely move in all its joints and was as strong and pliable as the real hand had been; and ever afterwards Nuada was known as *Argetlam*, the 'Silver Handed'. But it was a custom among the People of Danu that no man could rule over them whose body bore any sort of blemish, and so their leaders went into council to consider how best to choose a new king.

By now they knew the fearsome reputation of the malformed Fomorian giants who came from the sea. Always eager for a wise and peaceable settlement they decided it would be good to secure an alliance with them. Accordingly, ambassadors were sent to Elotha, king of the Fomors, asking him to give his son Breas to be the new ruler over the People of Danu.

Breas was Fomorian only on his father's side and therefore a handsome man by their hideous standards. When he accepted the offer gladly enough it was agreed that he should wed Brigid, daughter of the Dagda. Then the alliance between the two races was further strengthened by the wedding of Cian, son of the Danu physician Diancecht, to Eithne, who was the daughter of Balor of the Evil Eye.

Of the fruit of that marriage there are wonders still to tell; yet through this sealing of alliances all should have been well in Ireland, and might have been so had not the handsome Breas proved to be a cruel and greedy ruler.

Truer to his father's people than to those he now governed, the new king imposed heavy taxes on every hearth and trough and quern, as well as on the head of each one of the People of Danu. Nor did it end there. After they had agreed to yield as tribute to Breas the milk of those cows which were brown and hairless, the king craftily commanded that all the cattle in Ireland should be made to pass between two close fires, leaving every one of them burned brown and singed.

Soon even the great among the People of Danu were forced to labour to meet their king's demands while struggling to scrape a living of their own. Increasingly, hunger and cold became the lot of all, and the hungrier they grew the harder it was to perform the tasks expected of them. Even the once great strength of their champion Ogma was so depleted that he wearied himself gathering logs enough for the fire.

The great leader Dagda had been given the arduous task of building forts and castles for the king. While he sweated at his work, his son Aengus came to him one day saying, 'What reward will you ask of Breas when your work is done?'

'I have had no time to think of it,' said the Dagda.

'Then take my advice,' Aengus answered, 'and ask Breas to gather all the cattle of Ireland on a plain and let you choose just one of them for your own. He will consent to that.'

'And which one shall I choose?' asked his father.

'Choose the black-maned heifer which is called Ocean,' Aengus told him. 'You will not regret the bargain.'

When the Dagda had finished his task he did as his son had advised, and Breas laughed at what he took for the Dagda's simple-mindedness; yet a day would come when the wisdom of the choice would be clear to all.

Meanwhile times were hard, and in those hard times, Miach, another son of the physician Diancecht, came with his sister to the place where Nuada had retired after losing the throne. The doorkeeper at Nuada's hall was also a maimed man, having lost an eye in the same battle. When he challenged the two strangers on their approach, they claimed that they were good doctors who could easily replace his missing eye with the eye of a cat. The half-blind man was willing enough to let them practise their art on him, and so quickly and skilfully was the job done, that Nuada commanded the doctors to attend to his own wounds, where his flesh festered from the rubbing of the silver hand against the stump of his wrist.

Asking where Nuada's lost hand had been buried, Miach sent for it to be dug up again. Then he placed the severed hand at Nuada's stump and worked a powerful enchantment over the torn flesh. Within three days, hand and arm had knitted back together at the wrist again and the terrible wound was healed.

Two lesser stories were to grow from these events. Firstly, it is said that the doorman was not long pleased with his new eye because when he tried to sleep it stayed open all night long on the lookout for mice, and when he needed to keep watch by day the eye kept falling shut.

Nor did much good come to Miach from his marvellous skill at surgery. When Diancecht heard how his son had exceeded his own powers he was overwhelmed with rage. Three times he struck his intimate rival over the head with a sword, once through the skin, then to the bone, then right through to the brain itself. Yet each time Miach healed the wound, and only when a fourth blow clove his brain in two did he finally fall dead.

On the mound of his grave grew three hundred and sixty five herbs, capable of healing every ailment of the human body. His sister covered the ground with her mantle and patiently sorted these herbs across the cloth according to their sovereign properties. Because of her careful work men might now be free from all forms of mortal illness had not Diancecht in his ungovernable rage snatched the mantle away, thereby confusing all the precious herbs beyond recovery.

In the meantime, however, Nuada was whole once more. Nor could the healing have happened at a better time, for the people of Danu had grown weary of Breas and his oppressive ways. To the vice of his greed had been added the further insult of his meanness, and none was treated at his court with the liberality that becomes a king. For this reason he was to fall victim to the first satire that was ever written in Ireland.

This was the way of it.

Late one night Cairpre, a son of Ogma and chief bard of the People of Danu, came to the king's hall as if expecting to eat well at the royal table and then to be comfortably lodged. Instead he found himself fobbed off in a narrow, cheerless room with neither fire nor bed to comfort him and with only mean cakes of dry bread put out on a little dish for nourishment. When he left the next day the bard did so without singing the customary tribute of praise to his host.

In its place Breas heard Cairpre utter, in a voice loud enough for all to hear, this magical imprecation:

On the plates, no meat;
From the kine, no milk;
For the traveller, no bed;

For the bard, no reward:
May Breas himself enjoy such cheer
As comes to others at his hand!

So powerful was the public shame of these words that the face of Breas instantly broke out in a violent rash of sore boils. When the people of Danu saw this blemish on his person they demanded that he immediately stand down as king and let Nuada take back his throne. No longer able to command the assent of his subjects, Breas returned to the land of the Fomors where before an assembly of all the chiefs he urged his father, Elotha, to raise an army against the People of Danu and take Ireland back beneath the waves.

Restored to his throne, Nuada saw that war with the Fomorians must now be unavoidable, so he called together a council of his own at Tara, the high seat of the Irish kings.

All the great leaders of the People of Danu gathered at the feast to consider how the coming assault might best be countered. Then, when the debate was raging at its height, a stranger regally dressed in the garb of a warrior-king was seen approaching the gate.

The doorkeeper challenged the newcomer to state his name and tell what errand brought him to Tara.

'I am called Lugh,' the stranger replied. 'I am the grandson of Diancecht by my father Cian, and the grandson also of Balor the Fomorian by my mother Eithne. Moreover I was fostered to manhood by Taillte, daughter of the great magician Manannan mac Lir, lord of the great sea-plain.'

'That may be so,' said the doorkeeper, 'but only those who are masters of an art are allowed to enter Tara. What craft do you have at your command?'

'I am a carpenter,' Lugh answered, 'skilled in the mystery of building.'

'Luchtaine is already carpenter at Tara,' said the porter.

'Then I am a blacksmith,' Lugh returned at once.

'We already have an excellent smith. His name is Goibniu,' the porter replied.

'Then know that I am also an accomplished warrior.'

'Have you not heard that Tara already has a great champion in Ogma, brother to the king.'

'Then I am a harper,' said Lugh.

'We have a fine harper among us,' he was told.

'Yet am I a poet and storyteller also.'

'Tara is in need of neither,' said the doorkeeper. 'We have both among our number.'

'I have the powers of a magician,' said Lugh.

The porter merely shrugged. 'Is it not well known there are many powerful enchanters inside Tara?'

'I am a skilled healer also.'

'What need of that when Diancecht is our physician?'

'Then let me be a cupbearer.'

'There are nine cupbearers here already,' said the doorkeeper. 'What need for more?'

'Am I not also skilled at work in bronze?'

'Yet who does that better than our own brazier, Credne?'

'Then go to your king,' said Lugh at last, 'and ask if has in his company any man who is skilled in all the arts. If there is already such a man in Tara I shall not ask to enter again.'

When the doorkeeper went inside and reported that there was a stranger at the gate claiming to be master of all the arts known among the people of Danu he was met with scoffing laughter; but Nuada decided that the newcomer's extravagant claims must be put to the test.

'There has been no mention of fidchell[1],' he said. 'Let him sit at the gaming board with our best player.'

The board was brought out and from every game that was played Lugh emerged the victor, even inventing a new move that was ever afterwards called 'Lugh's Enclosure.'

When Nuada heard of this triumph he gave leave for Lugh to enter Tara because a man of so many accomplishments had never been seen in that company.

So Lugh came into the courtyard and took possession of the seat which was reserved for the greatest man of knowledge. As he did so he saw Ogma, champion of Tara, exerting all his mighty strength to lift a flagstone so heavy that four-score yokes of oxen might scarcely have shifted it. Rolling the stone across the yard, Ogma placed it outside the walls as a challenge to Lugh to match his show of strength.

Lugh got up from his seat in silence, passed back through the gate, lightly picked up the stone and tossed it over the wall so that it landed in the place where it belonged.

In awe of his many skills, the People of Danu asked Lugh to entertain them with the sound of his harp, which he gladly agreed to do. First he played them the drowsy-making music, which lulled the king and all his court into such untroubled sleep they did not wake again until the same hour on the next day. Then so plaintive were the strains of sorrowful music he plucked from his strings they were all left weeping. Their grief might have been

---

1 The word means 'wooden wisdom' and was the name of a board-game, perhaps similar to chess, in which two sets of men were pegged in competition across the board. To the Celts of Wales it was known as *gwyddbwyll*.

inconsolable had he not lastly made such spirited measures lift from his harp as left their hearts overflowing with joy.

Ever afterwards Lugh was hailed as *Samildanach*, Master of all the Arts.

It was evident to Nuada that such a gifted man must prove invaluable in the coming struggle against the Fomorian hosts. Taking counsel with the others, he decided it would be best for the kingdom if he were to yield up the throne to Lugh for the space of thirteen days until their plans were clear. So with Nuada sitting in the seat of knowledge beside him, Lugh took the throne and called the People of Danu into a war-council where he asked each of them what deeds they would perform in the fray.

Goibniu the smith spoke first. 'I will arm our men with spears that never miss their mark,' he said, 'and all the wounds that they give shall be mortal. And for every lance or sword that is broken I shall forge another even though this war should last for seven years. The smith of the Fomors cannot do as much. The outcome will be decided by my spears.'

'And I shall furnish the rivets for those spears,' said Credne the brazier, 'and I shall make hilts for the swords and rims for the bosses of our shields.'

'And it is I who shall shape those shields,' said the carpenter Luchtaine, 'and I will hew the wood to furnish shafts for those lances.'

'And my skill shall swiftly heal each of our men that is wounded,' said Diancecht, 'unless it be that that his spine is severed or his head cut off.'

'The king of the Fomors shall die at my hand, together with thrice nine of his warriors,' boasted Ogma the champion. 'Moreover a third of his army shall fall captive to me.'

'And you, Dagda,' demanded Lugh, 'what will you do in the battle?'

'I shall wield my club so mightily,' answered the Dagda, 'that wherever the two armies meet, the bones of our enemies will be crunched like hailstones under my horse's hooves.'

Then Lugh turned to the grey-haired Morrigan, the Crow of Battle, and to Mathgan, the head sorcerer, asking what their powers might achieve. 'I will pursue them when they flee,' said the Morrigan, 'and I always catch what I chase.'

'By our magic arts,' Mathgan promised, 'we sorcerers will turn the trees and sods and stones into armed men fighting on our side. We will hurl the twelve mountains of Ireland after the Fomors.'

Then, fired by the gathering ardour around them, the nine cup-bearers vowed that they would use their magic to conceal the twelve lakes and the twelve rivers of Ireland so that no matter how thirsty the Fomorian warriors became, nowhere would they find a trace of water to slake their thirst. Lastly the druid Figol swore that he would send streams of fire into the faces of the Fomors which would rob them of two parts of their strength and courage, while the people of Danu would grow stronger and more eager with every breath they drew.

So it was that all those gathered at Tara committed themselves to war with the terrible Fomorian people, and all assented that Lugh, grandson of both Diancecht the physician and Balor of the Evil Eye, should be first among them.

Preparations for the war lasted many years. For a time Lugh withdrew to take counsel with Nuada and the Dagda and the champion Ogma. They were joined by Diancecht and Goibniu in deliberations that were kept closely secret so that the Fomors would not learn of their plans till all was ready. Then Lugh returned to his friends among the people of Mananann mac Lir, and it was not till the tax-gatherers of the Fomors came to levy their dues at Balor's Hill that he was seen again.

Gleaming with the radiance of the sun, Lugh came galloping across the plain towards the Fomorian warriors. At his side rode his foster brothers, the sons of Mananann mac Lir, followed by the Riders from the Land of Promise that lies beneath the waves. Lugh was mounted on Mananann's own shining horse that could stride as easily over land as over sea and was swift as is the naked wind in spring. He was armoured in Mananann's own helmet and breastplate that would turn aside the point and edge of every weapon, and at his side swung Manannan's great sword, the Answerer, the plain sight of which sheared men of their strength, and from whose blows none ever escaped alive. When he reined in his horse and took off his helmet, the splendour of his forehead shone so brightly that the Fomors could not bring their gaze to bear on him. For this was Lugh Lamfada, the Far-Shooter, he of the long hand, the champion of the sun. With the speed of sunlight now, he and his company fell on the host of the tax-gatherers, killing all but nine of them, who were left to return to the dark land of the Fomors bringing their terrible news.

Among the chief warriors of the Fomors was Balor himself, Lugh's grandfather on his mother's side, he of the Evil Eye. Balor was so called because of the poisonous eye with which he had once spied on his father's sorcerers through a chink in a door. Bathed in the fumes rising from the magic potion they were brewing, the eye had been infected by their toxic power. Its glance at once became so deadly that the youth had been allowed to live only so long as that terrible eye was kept closed. Now it was opened only in time of need in battle, and it took the strength of four men to lift the brass ring on the lid that sealed its terrors shut.

'Who can this great warrior be?' Balor demanded when he heard how his tax-gatherers had been routed.

Only his wife knew the answer. 'Who else can be possessed of such powers but the son of our own daughter Eithne? And since he has chosen to fight beside his father's people, it is in my mind that the Fomors shall never rule in Ireland again.'

Yet once the full might of the People of Danu was gathered to meet the Fomorian host in the field, their leaders decided that Lugh's life was far too valuable to be risked in battle. Despite his protests, he was left behind under the guard of nine warriors when, on the eve of Samhain, Nuada and his army advanced to meet their enemies on the wide plain at Moytura.

It was the Morrigan who had first heard that the host of the Fomors had come ashore in Ireland. She immediately sent word to the Dagda who ordered his druids to utter their deadliest imprecations against them. Then, to gain time for the gathering of Nuada's host, the Dagda himself went into the camp of the Fomors under the pretence of parleying with them.

Now the Dagda had a reputation as a prodigious trencherman and the Fomors decided to make sport of it. In a cauldron deep as five giant's fists they prepared a great feast of porridge for him. Eighty gallons of milk were poured into the cauldron along with numerous sacks of meal and bacon-fat. To this rich mix they added the carcasses of goats and sheep and pigs, boiled the whole broth together and tipped it into a hole in the ground. Then they bade the Dagda come and eat his fill.

'We would not have you return to the People of Danu with complaints about our hospitality,' they said. 'So if a drop of it remains uneaten you shall lose your life.'

Licking his lips undaunted, the Dagda picked up a ladle big enough for a man and woman to lie together in the bowl of it, dipped it in the vat and sniffed. 'If the broth tastes as good as it smells,' he said, 'this should be tasty fare.'

He put the ladle to his mouth and took a sip from it which amounted to half a salted pig and a quarter of lard, and grunted his approval. Having begun, he carried on eating till every last scrap of the porridge was scraped from the ground. By that time his belly was bigger than the cauldron of a great house, and blown out like a great sail in the wind. So, followed by the coarse laughter of the Fomors, the Dagda staggered away to sleep off his meal. But valuable hours had been gained and all the host of his kinsmen was now assembled for the fight.

Rarely was battle more strangely fought than in that confict between the People of Danu and the Fomorian giants.

For a time the main armies looked on unmoving while individual soldiers, ambitious to make a name for themselves, rode out to give single combat. Each day the honours went from side to side: sometimes the People of Danu hailed their champion's return, sometimes the giants stood triumphantly beating their shields. But not many days had passed before the Fomorians began to notice that when the weapons of their men were broken they remained that way, while the smashed spears of their enemies were speedily repaired. Stranger still, when one of their own warriors fell dead that was the end of him, but the fallen heroes of the other side quickly came back to the field as if not a drop of their blood had ever been spilled.

It was decided that a spy must be sent to discover the secret of this mystery.

Ruadan was the chosen man. Being the son of Breas by the Dagda's daughter Brigid, he was able to pass himself off as one of the People of Danu. Entering their camp under the cover of darkness, he eventually came upon the smithy where Goibniu forged lance-heads with three swift blows, while Luchtaine as quickly hewed shafts for them, and Credne riveted them together with bronze nails that seemed to need no hammering.

Alarmed by what he'd seen Ruadan hastened back to the Fomorian lines with his unnerving news.

'What about the reviving of the dead?' Breas demanded.

'I saw nothing of that.'

Balor grunted. 'Yet about this magic forge something might be done,' he said, and shared his plan with Ruadan.

At dusk the next day Ruadan returned to Goibniu's smithy, presenting himself as a warrior with a damaged spear. The smith took the weapon from him, beat the broken head whole and handed it back to Ruadan, saying, 'Kill a Fomorian for me, friend.'

But as soon as Ruadan had the spear in his hands he lowered it and thrust its head through Goibniu's guts. He would have wrenched it out again but the smith resisted him, holding the shaft in his powerful grip. Disarmed, Ruadan turned to make his escape, and it was then that Goibniu pulled out the spear and hurled it against his assailant, giving him a mortal wound.

Ruadan dragged himself back to the Fomorian camp where he died before the eyes of his keening parents; but Goibniu took no great harm from this adventure. His bleeding corpse was carried to Diancecht who plunged it into the spring of healing and instantly the great gash through his guts was healed. The next day the smith was hammering at his anvil as vigorously as ever.

With such powerful enchantments on their side the People of Danu must soon have worn down the enemy host had not one of the Fomorians discovered the whereabouts of the healing spring.

He stood in the green shade of the trees some distance away, staring in amazement as Diancecht and his handmaidens submerged a smashed and bleeding body beneath the glassy surface, held it there for a time, singing charms that did not reach him clearly on the summer breeze, then lifted out the dazed figure of a mended living man. For a time the warrior stood spellbound at the mystery of the sight, then he hastened back to bring his news to Balor.

That warrior returned in the night bringing companions with him. Together they fetched great stones from the River Drowes and blocked the mouth of the wellspring with them until it was entirely covered by a cairn. Thereafter the People of Danu could no longer renew their numbers and, heartened by this sudden change in their own fortunes, the Fomors decided to commit their host to open battle.

All the great warriors of both armies were drawn up facing each other across the northern plain of Moytura, and things might have gone ill for the People of Danu had not Lugh sensed what was happening and managed to elude his guards that morning. Hastening to the field, he drove his chariot along the line, shouting words of encouragement that all might see and hear him.

The dazzle of light glancing off his armoured figure carried eastwards across the plain to the opposing lines. Seeing it, Breas turned to his druid and said, 'Is it not a strange wonder that the sun should rise in the west today when on every other day it rises in the east?'

Shaking his head, the druid answered, 'Would that it were truly so.'

'What else can such light be?' asked Breas, puzzled.

'It is the radiance that shines from the face of Lugh,' he was answered.

Then with a great shout the two armies fell upon each other, and so fierce and close was the fighting that the raging sound of it shook the ears of men with thunder and the ground ran thick and slippery with blood.

Chief after great chief fell in the struggle so that bodies lay piled on one another under the feet of the striving warriors on the plain. Nuada of the Silver Hand found his death that day at the hand of Balor of the Mighty Blows; and so did Nuada's warlike wife Macha, who had fought savagely at her husband's side. Then as the battle turned and rolled towards the banks of the river, Balor was confronted at last by his grandson, Lugh, who hurled a fearless challenge at him in the Fomorian speech he had learned at his mother's lap.

Angered by his defiance, Balor turned to his followers saying, 'Lift up my eyelid now that I might look upon this chatterer.'

It took four men to wield the great hook through the ring on Balor's eyelid, and had they raised it faster Lugh himself would have looked upon the light no more. But the champion had known what must happen and, when the terrible eye was still only half-open, he released from his sling that kind of magic stone which is called a *tathlum* in Ireland. The stone struck Balor's slowly opening eye with such violent force that it was driven out through the back of his skull. The eye fell on the ground, staring upwards, instantly killing a whole rank of Fomorian warriors who had the ill luck to be standing in its sight.

Lugh released his battle-roar and, shocked by the sudden blinding of Balor's evil eye, the whole line of the Fomors wavered in its advance.

Then the terrible She-crow of Battle, the Morrigan, was heard shrieking a song of triumph that brought new strength to the people of Danu and a pang of fear into the hearts of their foes. 'Kings, arise to battle,' she sang, and knowing that once the Morrigan gave chase, her quarry would fly like chaff before the wind, the *Tuatha de Danann* made a great push that broke the Fomor's line.

Once through there was no stopping them. The host of the Fomors fled before them and they were driven back across the plain, out over the shores of Ireland, and down to their own dark glades beneath the sea.

The handsome Breas, who had so abused his kingship over the people of Danu, was captured in that violent rout and brought before Lugh for judgement.

'You would do better to spare me than to kill me,' he said, pleading for his wretched life.

'Why?' Lugh answered. 'What ransom can you pay?'

'Do I not have the power to keep all the cattle of Ireland in milk?' Breas said.

Thinking on this, Lugh consulted with his druids but it was decided that what Breas had offered was not enough unless he also had power to lengthen the life of the cows. This Breas could not do; yet he had a further desperate offer to make.

'Spare my life,' he said, 'and I shall use my powers so that there will be a harvest in Ireland four times in every year.'

But the thought of all the work this would entail did not greatly please the People of Danu. 'We already have the spring for ploughing and sowing,' the Dagda said, 'we have the summer to ripen the crops, the autumn for reaping, and the winter to eat the bread. That is enough for us.'

'However,' Lugh added after a moment, 'you shall keep your life for a lesser thing than that.'

'And what is that?' Breas eagerly asked.

'If your knowledge of nature's increase is so great,' said Lugh, 'tell us on what day it is best for us to plough, on what day we should sow, and when we ought to reap.'

'You should plough on a Tuesday, sow on a Tuesday and reap on a Tuesday,' Breas replied, and for this parsimonious answer his life was spared as Lugh had promised it would be.

Nor did the chase of the Fomors end at the shores of Ireland. In their despoiling flight the giants had carried off the great harp that belonged to the Dagda, though it was of no use to them since its strings would not play without its owner's leave. So Lugh, Ogma and the Dagda followed Breas to the place beneath the waves where Elotha, king of the Fomors, ruled and there they saw the harp hanging on the wall.

Softly the Dagda called to the harp by its two names, 'Oak of the Two Cries' and 'Hand of Fourfold Music.' Instantly the harp leapt down from the wall killing nine of the Fomors in its flight.

As soon as the instrument was in his hand, the Dagda played the sorrowful music that set the Fomors weeping, then the joyful music that shook their sides with laughter, and lastly the drowsy music that put them all so soundly to sleep that he and Ogma and Lugh could steal away in safety from the Fomors' halls.

And after that the Dagda took back from the Fomors the black-maned heifer called Ocean, which he had obtained from Breas at the advice of his son Aengus. This was the very beast that the People of Danu followed whenever it lowed. Now, at the appearance of its master, the heifer lowed again, and all the cattle which the Fomors had stolen from the *Tuatha de Danann* answered that call and came back with the Dagda into Ireland.

Not all the power of the Fomors was broken, but the Morrigan's pursuit had driven them out of Ireland. It was she and the other great warrior-queens who proclaimed the victory from all the summits of Ireland.

It should have been a joyful moment, but a prophesy was made at that time that one age was coming to an end and another about to begin; and in the iron time which was to come summer would bring no flowers and the trees would bear no fruit. The cattle would yield no milk in that time, and there would be no fish in the sea. It was said also that in that age the women would be shameless and the men without heart, that judges would give false judgments and the lawgivers make bad laws, while those who had once been comrades would betray each other and there would be no virtue left in the world.

Yet before the coming of that dreadful time Lugh ruled as king in Ireland for forty years. He had two wives, one called Bui, the other Nas, and it was in their honour that he founded the August festival of *Lughnasadh* which bears the name of Lugh's Commemoration to this day.

Some say that Lugh met his end at Uisneach, the place at the centre of Ireland where the five provinces meet and the first fire was kindled in Ireland. It was there he was speared in the foot by the sons of Cearmaid, whose father he had slain. They say that the wounded Lugh retreated to the lake where he was drowned, and which was named for him afterwards as Loch Lughbortha.

But others say that he was seen in Ireland again at the time of King Conor and the Men of the Red Branch, and that it was none other than Lugh himself that kept watch over Cuchullain while he slept for three days at the time of the cattle raid of Cuailnge.

There is yet another story which tells how Conn was in Tara at one time and he chanced to stand on a stone in the sacred enclosure which let out a great scream. When Conn asked his chief druid about this strange event, he learned that it was the Stone of Destiny which the people of Danu had brought with them out of Falias.

While Conn and the druid stood in that place a dark mist wrapped itself round them and they saw a great rider come out of the mist who cast three spears at them. Then they were transported to a beautiful plain where stood a king's dun with a golden tree at its gate, and inside the dun was a fine house with a roof of bronze. The rider was waiting for them there.

He sat in the royal seat of the house, a man fairer than any in Ireland at that time, and with the lucid, awesome dignity of a great lord about him. Beside him waited a young woman with a gold band in her hair who kept a silver vessel filled with red ale near to hand, together with its bowl and cup.

'Whom shall I serve with this?' she asked her lord.

'Serve it to Conn of the Hundred Battles,' he answered, 'for this man shall win a hundred battles before he dies.'

Then the ale was also poured out for Conn's son whose name was Art of The Three Shouts, and the lord listed the names of all those who would be king in Ireland after that time and told how long each of their reigns would last.

When the chalice was emptied the maiden lifted it again and solemnly presented it to Conn together with its gleaming bowl and cup. As Conn stood in breathless gratitude holding these treasures at his chest, the lord smiled at him and told him that the maiden who had yielded those things over to his hand was none other than the Sovereignty of Ireland.

'And as for myself,' he added, 'I am Lugh the Long-handed, Master of all the Arts.'

2

The Sorrows of Deirdre

At the time of this story the kingdom of Ulster stretched as far south as the River Boyne and was ruled by Conor mac Nessa, the last of its great kings. One night Conor was invited to a feast of celebration in the house of the king's storyteller, Fedlimid, the son of Dall. The king's druid Cathbad was there at his side and all the chief warriors of the Red Branch were gathered among that jovial company. So copious was the food and so swiftly were the drinking horns refilled that it was not long before a loud drunken hubbub resounded through the hall.

Fedlimid's wife was far gone in pregnancy at the time but she served at the table nevertheless, working hard to feed the lively appetites of her guests and making sure they lacked for nothing. But as the night wore on and the revellers showed no sign of retiring, the woman suddenly felt faint and knew that she needed to lie down. Making her apologies she quietly left the feast, but had not been gone from the room for more than a few moments when the whole company was shocked to silence by the sound of her baby shrieking inside her womb.

The strange cry caused such consternation among the drunken guests they demanded to know what such an unnatural event might mean. So Fedlimid's wife was brought back into the hall and the wan-faced, anxious woman turned for comfort to Cathbad the druid, who was a seer. Gazing into her eyes for some time, then closing his own, Cathbad went into a prophetic state of trance from which he sang:

In the cradle of this womb cries
A woman of flowing golden hair.
Her eyes are deep-searching grey,
Her cheeks the hue of foxgloves,
And behind vermilion lips lie
Teeth immaculate as fresh-fallen snow.
Among the chariot-men of Ulster
She will cause much slaughter.

Then he opened his eyes again and put his hand to the woman's belly. Feeling how the unborn infant stormed in its waters at the touch of his hand, he said, 'Truly this is a girl-child. Her name shall be Deirdre. Great evil will come of her.'

Hearing the druid's words, Fedlimid's wife moaned and swooned and went immediately into labour. Not long afterwards the child was born.

Listening to the birth pangs and the cries of the newborn babe, the warriors of the Red Branch murmured amongst themselves about the druid's prophecy and this ill-aspected birth. Sobered by the events of the night, it was clear to them that the wisest course was to have the fateful child killed at once before harm could come of it. They said as much to the king himself but Conor would not hear of it. Sensing a destiny of his own in the child's vivid eyes, he declared that he would have the infant concealed in a remote place known only to himself where she would be raised as his companion.

Though they were dismayed by the decision, none of the Red Branch warriors dared oppose it, so the child was taken from her mother at birth and brought away to a secluded place in the wilds of Ulster. Conor appointed foster parents to nurse and raise her, and no one else would have known where Deirdre was hidden had not the powerful poet and satirist, Leborcham, made plain her demand that the child must have a teacher and that she herself was the one to give instruction.

In that chosen company, with all else excluded from her sight, the child grew up until all the delicate beauty that Cathbad had prophesied was seen in her face, and Conor learned that she must soon become the loveliest woman in all Ireland.

One winter's day Deirdre's foster father slaughtered a calf to roast over the open fire outside their bothy. As the young woman stood watching him skin the carcass, a raven swooped down from a near-by tree to sip at the blood in the snow. Deirdre's eyes were drawn by the sudden vivid contrast of colours – against the radiant white snow the blood glistened more brightly and the sheen of the raven's plumage seemed more glossily black. For a long time she stood in a trance-like gaze, until Leborcham came up beside her to ask what fancy had so possessed her thoughts.

'A man whose hair was black as the raven's back,' Deirdre whispered, 'and whose cheeks were as red as the calf's blood, and whose body was as white and clear as the snow... If one were to see such a man he would seem fair indeed!'

'Bless your heart,' said Leborcham with a casual laugh, 'you need look no further than the nearest settlement for such a man. Naoise, one of the sons of Usnech, looks exactly like that.'

'Then I shall not be well again,' said Deirdre, 'till I have looked on him for myself.'

Ruing her own thoughtless impulse, the bard told her that she must put such idle fancies from her mind; but the vision that had possessed Deirdre was not so easily dispelled. As she sat pining alone one day it occurred to her that the faint call sometimes borne on the wind across the valley must come from Usnech's settlement. The next time it rang in her ears she decided to follow the gentle sound to its source.

It was the call that Naoise gave from the rampart-mounds of his father's dwelling to call the cattle home. So sweet was that call it soothed the cows into increasing their milk and lightened the hearts of all who heard it. Now, with her own heart trembling like a moth, Deirdre approached the rampart where Naoise sat amongst some Ulstermen passing the time of day. She walked with her eyes averted, pretending she had not noticed him there. Astonished by this beautiful girl he had never seen before, Naoise turned to his friends and said loudly enough for her to hear, 'It's a fair heifer that passes me by this day.'

On a sudden wing of inspiration Deirdre replied, 'The heifers grow fairest where there are no bulls.'

'There are young bulls enough in these parts,' Naoise answered lightly, alert to the promise in her voice.

'Yet the King of Ulster himself will not let me come near them,' said Deirdre, and gazed up at the young man so that for the first time he saw the full beauty of her face.

In that moment Naoise knew two things: he knew that his heart was irretrievably lost and he knew who the girl must be. His agitated heart was trembling as he said, 'Then you have the greatest bull in Ulster at your bidding,' and looked away.

Deirdre shrugged and sighed. 'Yet if I had to choose between that great bull and a younger, I would choose the one more like yourself.'

Swallowing, Naoise shook his head, his limbs shaking. 'Then I think you would bring great harm on that young man,' he said. 'Did not Cathbad the druid foretell it so?'

Deirdre looked back at him then with eyes that searched his soul so deeply he could scarcely stand under their gaze.

'Would you reject me for that reason?' she demanded.

'I would,' Naoise answered hoarsely and would have turned away again but before he knew what was happening, Deirdre had sprung forward, grey eyes flashing with incredulous rage, and grabbed him hard by both ears. 'Then here are two fool's ears of shame,' she cried, tugging at them fiercely before pulling away, white with passion, holding him in her gaze. 'And I cry derision on your name, Naoise son of Usnech, if you lack the heart to follow your destiny and carry me out of Ulster.'

With his ears ringing, hot with the humiliation of being shamed before his friends, Naoise stood transfixed by her words. Then one of his companions muttered a rough joke at his expense and with a great angered roar of indignation Naoise threw himself on the lad. Already excited by Deirdre's ardent beauty, the whole bunch of them were suddenly on their feet, throwing blows at each other until the din was so loud that Usnech and his other sons came out, shouting to calm them down and demanding to know the cause of all this trouble.

As Deirdre stood proudly by the rampart with her chin tipped skywards at his words, Naoise told his father what had happened and how the woman had put the curse of her derision on him if he did not carry her away. For the first time Usnech brought himself to look at Deirdre and felt his own heart shake at the impact on his senses. Seeing that his son was loved by a woman that any man might readily die for, he shook his head and murmured, 'Nothing but evil can come of this. It is as Cathbad prophesied.'

'Yet we cannot let our name be shamed,' insisted one of Naoise's brothers, Ardan; and then, less certainly, 'And the woman is beautiful. It were a great pity to let her go.'

'Then it seems we must choose between Cathbad's doom and a beautiful woman's cursing,' said the other brother, Ainle.

'And what of you, Naoise?' Usnech demanded. 'This is of your making. What do you have to say in this?'

Conscious that Deirdre's grey, reproachful eyes were on him demanding truth, Naoise stood in silence for a time. He knew that his entire life stood in the balance now.

'The woman has vowed that if she had to choose between Conor King of Ulster and myself,' he said, 'then she would choose me; and the heart inside me leapt to hear that word.' Breathing quickly but smiling with sudden tender recognition, he went on, 'And I myself – if I have to choose between a life at peace without Deirdre beside me, and a fugitive life that honours the love that is alive between us now, then it is Deirdre and exile that I choose, whether my kinsmen will join me in it or no.'

Usnech listened in silence as his son uttered these words, and when Deirdre herself spoke of the vision that had caused her to seek out Naoise with such unquestioning certainty, he saw that a powerful, supervening destiny of love such as few are ever granted had come upon the two young people standing before him now. For good or ill they must accept it.

'Yet Conor will not let us keep her in Ulster,' he said.

'Conor is not loved elsewhere,' Ardan said. 'There's not a king in Ireland who will refuse us shelter against him.'

So that very night they gathered all their clan together and carried Deirdre away with them out of Ulster.

Not long afterwards Leborchan returned to Emain Macha to face Conor's fury. When the woman told him of Deirdre's flight with Naoise, the impassioned king swore that his mind would know no peace till he had taken vengeance. He went far beyond his own borders in search of them. Usnech and his sons were harried from kingdom to kingdom throughout Ireland until the father died from the weariness of their life, and Naoise and his brothers saw that they too would have no peace unless they could make a life with Deirdre beyond the shores of Erin.

So they took ship for Alba where for a time they made a sparse living, hunting and cattle-rustling among the glens; but everywhere they went men were so excited by Deirdre's beauty that Usnech's kinsmen went in constant fear of their lives.

At last, in a bid for security, they put themselves in service to a Scottish king, building a hamlet of huts in his meadow where Naoise tried to keep his wife hidden from sight.

But such luminous beauty will not stay hidden long. When the king's steward was making his rounds of the hamlet early one morning he came on Naoise and Deirdre tenderly asleep in each other's arms and was staggered by the sight of the woman's naked loveliness. Rushing immediately back to the court, he roused his royal master with the news that at last he had found a woman worthy to be the wife of the King of the Western World. She was living among his vassals in the house of Naoise, son of Usnech. 'And no king could ask for a fairer queen,' he urged. 'Have her husband killed and take the woman for your own.'

Such was the fateful power of Deirdre's beauty that Naoise might have found his death that way; but having taken Usnech's clan under his protection the king would not lightly contemplate such treachery. Instead he sent the steward to try to woo Deirdre away from her husband, offering a queen's throne for her desertion. But Deirdre desired no other life than the one she shared with Naoise, and at the steward's first approach she sent him coldly away with the message that nothing less than death would ever separate her from Naoise. Thereafter the king set about arranging that death by sending the sons of Usnech out into fierce skirmishes with his enemies; but the brothers returned unharmed and triumphant from every fight.

Yet Deirdre knew that the king would never give up till Naoise was dead. She begged him to take flight, and so the clan of Usnech moved on again. Unsafe in either Erin or Alba now, they found refuge on one of the remote western isles.

So the years passed by without Conor finding his vengeance. One night he was feasting drunkenly with the men of the Red Branch in Emain Macha when he demanded out loud to know whether any of them had ever heard of a nobler company than themselves. To a man they shouted that nowhere else in the world was such a valiant band to be found.

'And yet,' said the king unexpectedly, 'it weighs heavily on my heart that three of the bravest among our number are not here. Was it not once said that when the ardour of battle came on them the sons of Usnech could defend all Ulster alone, with help from none other? It is a great grief to me that they should have lived in banishment from our gatherings for all these years because a mere woman has come between us.'

Surprised and relieved by this conciliatory turn of feeling, those closest to Conor ventured to say that they too had often grieved at the thought.

'Then gladly would I have them back in Ulster,' the king declared. 'We will send sureties to them for their safe return. Surely one of our greatest champions will have the honour of bringing them home.'

Smiling, he looked around the table then, tapping it with his fingers as he measured each of the heroes gathered about him through narrowed eyes. 'Who shall it be – Conall the Victorious perhaps? Or Cuchullain son of Sualtam? Or the noble Fergus son of Roy?' He shook his drunken head, threw up his hands, laughed. 'How can a king choose among such champions?' Then he sat a while, pondering the problem before grunting with satisfaction. 'I shall send the one who loves me best.'

Then he withdrew with Conall secretly for a time and asked that champion what he would do if he were asked to bring the sons of Usnech back to Ulster under safe-conduct, only to see them cut down on their arrival.

'Were that to happen,' Conall answered quietly, 'I should see to it that not one of those involved in the treachery came out of it alive.'

Conor nodded at that, saying that Conall was an honourable man and he was glad of it but it was possible that others loved their king more. Then he dismissed him and called Cuchullain into his private chamber to answer the same question.

Fearing nothing and no one, the great champion answered, 'If such a thing were to happen by your command, Conor mac Nessa, I would accept no lesser compensation for the shame on my name than the sight of your own head swinging at my chariot-rail.'

'Have no fear of it,' said Conor. 'I expected no other answer and would never ask such a thing of you.'

Lastly the king called Fergus son of Roy into his presence and said, 'I would have you go as my emissary to the sons of Usnech and bring them back to Ulster.' Fergus declared that he valued the king's trust and would gladly serve him so.

'Yet there is a thing that troubles me,' Conor said.

'What thing is that?' asked Fergus.

'There are some hotheads about me here in Emain Macha. Out of a mistaken desire to prove their love they might still try to kill Naoise and his brothers on their return.'

'They would have to kill me first.'

'Good,' said Conor. 'But suppose you were not there to prevent it? What would you do then?'

'I would find the murderers and do swift justice on them.'

'Good,' Conor said. 'And on myself also?' he asked. 'If the deed were done in my name?'

Fergus frowned at the difficult thought. 'The king cannot be held accountable for every fool in Ulster,' he said. 'I would not seek redress on you.'

Then Conor smiled and thanked Fergus for his love.

Naoise was gaming at the fidchell board with his brother Ainle when they heard a shout carried on the wind up over the cliff.

'That was the voice of an Ulsterman,' said Naoise; but Deirdre who had heard it too and felt her heart suddenly fill with cold foreboding, said it was only the cry of a local fisherman and they should ignore it.

'I'm sure it was an Ulsterman's call,' Naoise insisted and sent Ardan to go and look.

Seeing an Irish galley in the cove, Ardan went down to the shore to get word of its purpose. After a time he saw Fergus striding ashore through the shallows between his two sons with Conor's own son, Cormac, bringing up the rear. He would have made his way quickly back up the cliff to warn his brothers had not Fergus shouted out at once that his intentions were peaceful and his news good.

That night around a simple feast-fire, Fergus sought to persuade the sons of Usnech that their tribulations were over and the time had now come to return to Ulster.

'And what of Conor's desire for vengeance?' Naoise asked.

'The years pass,' said Fergus, 'a man grows older, his passions cool. With my own ears I heard Conor rue your absence at the feast in Etain Macha. He repents grievously that the love of a woman should ever have come between you.'

'And why should I believe that,' Naoise answered, 'when he has harried me and my brothers across all Ireland?'

'Because you know me for a man of my word,' said Fergus. 'So sure am I of Conor's honesty in this, I have sworn to give my own two sons, Illann the Fair and Buinne the Red, in surety for your safe passage.'

'I have never had cause to doubt you or your sons,' said Naoise, 'but Conor has been no friend to me or my kin.'

'And he knows you have cause to doubt *him* therefore,' Fergus responded smiling. 'For which reason he sends his own son Cormac to be held in surety too. What fairer terms could a wronged king give than that?'

With this reminder that all the fault in the matter did not lie on Conor's side, the Ulsterman held out his open hands. 'Unless you wish to live out your days in such barren crofts as this I beg you to return with me to Ulster,'

When Naoise still hesitated, Fergus sighed saying, 'If you spurn Conor's friendship now he will not offer it again.'

So the sons of Usnech withdrew to confer together and were soon agreed that they should take advantage of this unexpected gesture of reconciliation.

Only Deirdre, who had stood apart throughout, listening but saying nothing, demurred. She had long since learned to curse her own beauty for the way it maddened the hearts of men, and she saw deeper into those hearts because of it. 'We have a life here in these peaceful glens,' she said. 'What more do we need than what we have? I fear for what will happen if we come back into Conor's power.'

But Usnech's sons had often yearned for the manly comradeship of the Red Branch Hall and the life they had forsaken in Ulster. The sight of Fergus and his sons had reminded them of all they had lost to keep Deirdre at Naoise's side. Insisting now that with Conor's own son hostage in their hands they were secure against treachery, they told her it was time to go home.

On the night before they sailed Deirdre sang a long lament for the life they were leaving, for their remote island refuge and the lovely glens of Alba where she and Naoise had lived in passionate simplicity together like a stag and a hind. She sang of nights when they had slept beneath the cliff, of the sea-sounds there, of the shining fish they had caught, the game they had chased across the moors and the wild garlic blowing in the brakes. She sang of the houses and cattlefolds they had built and left, and how her heart would have allowed her to leave none of this had not the man she loved asked it of her.

As they boarded the Irish galley and made sail for Ulster, the stirring sound of Deirdre's lament hovered in the hearts of the sons of Usnech softer than the falling rain.

In the very hour when they made landfall in Ulster, a message came from a local lord called Borrach inviting Fergus to a feast. Now Fergus was under a sacred prohibition that forbade him ever to refuse such an invitation, yet neither his own sons nor the sons of Usnech had been invited to Borrach's hall and he was uncertain what to do. Had he known that Conor's cunning hand was in the matter his mind might have been clearer, but that knowledge was withheld from him, so he turned to Naoise for advice.

'As for myself,' said Naoise, 'I shall eat no food in Ulster till I come to Conor's court. I am not offended that Borrach does not invite me to his hall.'

But still Fergus was in some perplexity, torn between his duty and his prohibition. At last Deirdre turned her searching eyes on him. 'If the destiny that has been laid on you is stronger than your duty to the sons of Usnech,' she said, 'then there is no avoiding it and you will do what is asked of you.'

At last Fergus left angrily for Borrach's feast, instructing Cormac and his sons to deliver Deirdre, Naoise and his brothers safely to Emain Macha with all speed. As soon as he had gone Deirdre gave a fearful little moan, swayed on her feet and swooned into a trance of dreadful visions. She saw a cloud of blood hovering over all their heads. Then she saw her husband Naoise and his brothers Ardan and Ainle dead and beheaded before her. She saw the lopped-off heads of Fergus's sons lying beside them in the dirt. Delirious with fear, she begged the men to take refuge in some safe retreat until Fergus returned from the feast. But Cormac, Illan and Buinne impatiently insisted that they must push on as Fergus had bidden them; and with Ardan and Ainle standing ill at ease beside him, Naoise tried to comfort his wife and laugh away her irrational fears.

Plead as she might Deirdre could not make them believe what she had seen. So they travelled on to Emain Macha where the gates stood open in welcome for them, and all seemed well when they learned that Conor had ordered the hall of the Red Branch to be made available for the comfort of his guests.

At that time, Conor was celebrating a recent triumph over Durthacht of Fermanagh by feasting that king's son, Eoghan, who had come to sue for peace. Somewhere in his mind was the thought that Eoghan might be useful to him in the unfolding of his plan, but first there was a matter preying on his mind that he needed to know.

That evening Conor summoned Leborchan and told her to visit Deirdre in her chamber and bring back a report of whether the woman was still as beautiful as she had been all those years ago when the old bard had taught her in the wilds of Ulster. Suspecting treachery, and bitterly aware of her own culpable role in the unfolding tragedy, Leborchan went into the hall of the Red Branch, fondly embraced Deirdre and warned the sons of Usnech of her fears. She promised to do what she could to help them with her lies, and when she went back to Conor told him that the hard years of enduring a fugitive life among the glens of Alba had left their mark on Deirdre's once fair face. 'Even such beauty as Deirdre once had is a fading thing,' she said. 'The girl you knew grew grey with care a long time ago. The haggard woman I saw tonight would not excite your heart.'

Conor nodded at that. His jealousy suddenly seemed a useless and pathetic thing. He himself was no longer the man he had once been, and the cares of age, the knowledge of what was for ever gone, and grief for his own lost youth weighed down his heart. He dismissed Leborchan from his presence and turned in gloomy, maudlin humour to drink himself into a stupor with Durthacht's darksome son, Eoghan.

Yet the longer he thought about it the more something in the old woman's face had bothered him, as if she had been a little too eager to confirm his fears, a little too gratified by his disenchanted acceptance of her report. Leborchan had once betrayed his trust. Might she not do so again?

Shaking his head clear, Conor shouted at the drowsy serving man by his chair to stir himself and go and peer in at the window of Deirdre's apartment.

'Tell me whether that old witch lied or not,' he said. 'Bring me back the truth of what you see.'

A few moments later Deirdre looked up from where she sat, in a trance of anxiety, watching Naoise and Ardan laughing over the gaming board. Having been gazed at by men all her days her senses knew when it was happening. She turned her head towards the window and saw the face of a man staring at her wide-eyed, his gap-toothed mouth agape with wonder.

Instinctively she leapt to her feet, snatched up one of the stone pieces from the gaming board and hurled it at the spy with all her might. The heavy piece struck him directly in one eye, leaving it blinded ever after; but the man had seen enough. With a hand held to the bleeding socket he hastened back to the king, saying that though Deirdre had robbed him of an eye, her beauty had already blinded him to all other women.

For an instant it was as though the words struck Conor with the stunning force of a blow. Then he rose drunkenly to his feet, reeling from the power of his rage, and shouted to the men around him that he wanted the hall of the Red Branch burned to the ground. When the men protested that Fergus's sons were lodged in the hall with Deirdre and the sons of Usnech, he said only, 'Let them all burn alive in there save Deirdre alone.'

Then he turned to Eoghan saying, 'If your father truly loves me now, you will aid me in this business.'

Uncertainly the men approached the hall with firebrands, but when the first torch was flung into the thatch, Fergus's son Buinne came out and swiftly extinguished the flames. He was joined a moment later by his brother Ilann and with cries of 'treachery', they drew their swords, preventing any further close approach to the hall.

Seeing that they meant to give resistance, Conor tried to buy them off with bribes and promises, but in the name of their father's honour, they refused. So the king armed his son Fiacha with his own magic weapons and sent him into the hall of the Red Branch with Eoghan at his side and a band of armed men after them to bring death into that place.

Among the arms which Conor had given his son was his great shield, the 'Moaner'. It was given that name because of a magical property which made it bellow for aid whenever its wielder was endangered. With that shield on his arm Fiacha rushed to meet Ilann and the two fought with fearsome violence until Conor's son slipped and fell to the ground, losing his grip on his sword. At once the great shield began to moan.

Conall the Victorious had been woken by the sounds of tumult from the Red Branch Hall. Arming himself he rushed out into the night where his ears were drawn by the baleful sound of Conor's shield. When he ran to help, all he could see in the gloom was a fallen man desperately trying to defend himself from the sword of an unidentifiable assailant. So thinking the king's own life was in danger, Conall hurled his spear into Ilann's stomach.

When he found that he had given a mortal wound to the son of his friend Fergus, the bewildered champion bent to comfort the youth and learned from his dying lips the truth of what was happening. Filled with rage at finding himself unwittingly drawn into such treason, Conall turned on Fiacha and cut him down before his father's eyes.

Across the courtyard Buinne already lay dead and beheaded at Eoghan's hand, but the resistance of Fergus's sons had given Naoise and his brothers time to fortify themselves inside the hall. With Conor grieving over his dead son, and dismayed confusion throughout the drunken hall of Emain Macha, the rest of that terrible night passed in an uneasy state of truce.

By dawn Naoise saw that their position inside the Red Branch Hall could not be held for long. Conor had already shown that if they remained inside, he was not above burning the thatch about their heads. It was clear that they must either break out through the ring of warriors surrounding them or die where they were. So he and his brothers formed a defensive wall about Deirdre with their shields and advanced into the day.

The men who faced them remembered in trepidation how Conor himself had once said that in their full battle ardour, the sons of Usnech could defend all Ulster on their own unaided. And Conor, too, must have feared that they would fight their way out of his grasp again because he had called on the druid Cathbad to add the power of magic to the force of arms.

So it was that as Naoise and his brothers saw the Ulstermen fall back, the bright day began to swirl and alter until the whole of Emain Macha seemed to be lurching unstably about them. Everything turned fluid and insubstantial at first, then it gathered a dense heaving strength until they felt themselves being tossed in the rising swell of a stormy sea.

With the tempest breaking over his head Naoise reached for Deirdre, holding her at his shoulder as he tried to keep both their heads above the breaking waves. Yet the weight of the breakers began to crash over them ever more heavily until all three gasping warriors flung aside their weapons in a desperate effort to stay afloat and swim.

Untouched by Cathbad's magic, Conor and his warriors looked on in amazement at the strange sight of three men and a woman of wondrous beauty striving to swim across dry land. In the moments before the enchantment that Cathbad had put upon them faded, the sons of Usnech were seized in their confusion and brought helplessly before the king.

Seeing the dark glower of triumph in Conor's eyes, Cathbad the druid said, 'Remember you vowed that if I worked this magic you would not take their lives, Conor.'

But the king merely gave a grim smile and said, 'And I will keep that word. I will not take their lives. Why should I when there are those here who will do it for me?'

Yet when Conor turned to the men of Ulster not one of them would act as his executioner. So Conor called forth the King of Fermanagh's son, saying, 'As your father loves me, Eoghan, you will do this thing for me.'

Held in Conor's unrelenting gaze, Eoghan stood silently a moment then nodded his head.

At that, Ardan said that he could not bear to see his brothers slain before his eyes and demanded that his own head be severed first. But Ainle protested that his grief would be just as great and offered his own neck to the blow.

Releasing Deirdre from his embrace with a last wan smile of farewell, Naoise stepped forward then and said, 'My brothers and I will die together as we have lived together. The sword I was holding is the "Retaliator". It was given to me at the hand of Manannan mac Lir and is strong enough to sever three heads at once. Strike cleanly, Eoghan.'

Then the sons of Usnech knelt side by side, and with a single stroke Eoghan sent their heads rolling in the dust.

By such treacherous deceits Conor avenged himself on the men who had taken Deirdre from him, but his triumph would not long endure for his closest followers were appalled by the contrast between his base guile and the noble end of the sons of Usnech. When Fergus returned from Borrach's feast to find his sons dead, Naoise, Ardan and Ainle murdered, and himself the dupe of Conor's stratagems, he raised his own kinsmen against the king. Three hundred Ulstermen died in the conflict. Fergus himself took the life of Conor's son, then went into exile to join Ulster's most powerful enemies at the court of King Ailill and Queen Maeve in Connaught.

Most daunting of all, Cathbad the druid called down his curses on the treacherous king, prophesying that none of Conor's line would rule again in Emain Macha. With the death of Ulster's greatest champion, Cuchullain, that prophesy would prove true.

And what of Deirdre?

The grief that overwhelmed the lovely, fate-afflicted woman as her terrible vision realized itself around her, found voice in the lament she made for the Sons of Usnech that night:

Long will be the day without Usnech's sons.
There was no sorrow in their company,
Those children of an open-handed man.

Three lions of the hills they were
Three hawks hovering above Slieve Gullion
Three men beloved of Alba's women.

Let none suppose that I will long survive
The death of my fair husband Naoise.
After three deaths another death shall not be long.

Three who never shrank from fight they were,
Three whom hardship never wearied
Three who bravely died together as they fought.

Oh you who make the grave for Naoise,
Dig it both deep and wide, for Deirdre
will lie beside her noble-hearted man.

Some say that she cheated Conor of his triumph by keeping that word and dying that very night. Others put a different end to her story, saying that the sorrows of Deirdre were prolonged throughout another year.

It was a year during which she never smiled or lifted her head from her knee. When Conor sent musicians in to charm her grieving soul, Deirdre would say, 'The music is sweet, but sweeter to me was the sound of Naoise's cry across the glen.'

And when Conor sought to comfort her, she turned away saying, 'You have taken from me what was dearest to me under the sky, and such are my sorrow and tears that I shall never love you till the day I die. If you had a heart to understand these things you would know that grief is stronger than the sea.'

He continued to press her, reminding her that from the moment of her birth she owed her very life to him, and that the first betrayal had been against himself.

'If I can forgive the wrong you have done to me,' he said, 'why can you not find it in your heart to end these sorrows by forgiving me and becoming my wife, as was first intended all those many years ago?'

'I have a husband,' Deirdre answered, 'whom I shall shortly join. I will never know two husbands together in this life.'

Eventually Conor lost patience with a woman whose implacable sorrow had begun to outweigh her beauty in his mind. Having suffered the humiliation of another cold rebuff, he said, 'There is too much hatred in your heart, Deirdre. Tell me, of all things in the world which do you hate most?'

'Yourself,' she answered at once, 'and Eoghan son of Durthacht.'

'Then your days shall be shared between us,' Conor answered grimly. 'Let Eoghan listen to your lamentations for a year!'

The next day the host assembled in parade on the plain outside Emain Macha. At his own hand the king delivered Deirdre up to stand beside Eoghan in his war-chariot. As he watched the chariot drive away, Conor saw her last disdainful glance and shouted after her, 'I think you are making the eye of the ewe between two rams, Deirdre!'

But Deirdre cried back, 'Did I not vow I would never know two husbands together in this life, Conor?' Then, as the king watched, she released her grip on the rail of the speeding chariot and hurled herself head-first against a huge rock by the road. In that moment both the great beauty and the great sorrows of Deirdre passed for ever from the earth.

3

The Cattle Raid of Cuailnge

Many heroes lived in the land of Ulster but of all their number none was greater than the warrior Cuchullain. His usual appearance was of a man of fine, fair stature, but when he was roused to the full height of his battle ardour, powerful changes would come upon him. At that time he would swivel round inside his skin; one of his eyes would swell to immense size while the other shrank inside its socket like a snail; and as his heart began to thunder inside the cage of his chest, his whole body burned as bright as a balefire. So fierce was the heat of it that snow would melt for a distance of thirty feet all about him. His flesh would hiss if he dipped it in the sea. None could bear to look upon Cuchullain when the frenzy of this transformation came upon him, for wrathful showers of sparks would blow from his mouth, his hair grew tangled as any thorn bush, and from the very crown of his head would spurt a tall plume of blood which gave off a shining pall of mist, like the smoke that billows over a royal house when a king draws near through winter light at nightfall.

The manner of Cuchullain's birth was attended by great wonders. His mother, Dechtire, was already at the table of her wedding feast with Sualtam, a chieftain of Ulster, when a mayfly flew unobserved into her cup and she drank it down. Then she fell into a deep sleep and the god Lugh came to her in a dream, saying that it was he in the mayfly that she had swallowed, and she was to leave the feast at once and come away with him, bringing fifty maidens with her.

By his magic art, Lugh put the shape of birds on the maidens and no one saw them leave. Nothing more was heard of the women until nine months later when a company of warriors was drawn out to go hawking after a shining flock of birds.

They followed their flight till nightfall, when they came to the place by the River Boyne where the gods have their home. A handsome man of noble bearing welcomed them into his palace, and in its great hall they found a beautiful woman waiting for them. She was attended by fifty maidens at a table filled with such a bounteous feast. After eating and supping to their heart's desire, the Ulstermen lodged in the palace that night. Far into the hours of darkness they were woken from sleep by the first vigorous cry of a newborn child.

The next morning the noble lord identified himself as the god Lugh. He declared himself to be father of the babe and told the huntsmen that the mother was Dechtire, half-sister to Conor mac Nessa who ruled in Ulster at that time. He commanded them to take the child back into the world with them and raise him as a warrior in Ulster. So the huntsmen returned to Conor's court at Emain Macha, bringing infant, mother and attendant maidens home with them, and the marriage between Dechtire and Sualtam was celebrated at last.

Sualtam warmly took the boy for his own son, and later one of Ulster's greatest warriors, Fergus son of Roy, stood foster father to him as was the custom among those people. But all the champions, bards, lawgivers and druids of Ulster vied with one another to have a hand in the education of the child that Lugh himself had sired.

At first they named the boy Setanta, but that was not to be the name by which his fame was known, and there is a story about the prodigious deed through which he won a name for himself.

As a child he was already so much stronger than the other boys that he could take them all on at the game of hurley single-handed. One day Conor the King rode by with the warriors of the Red Branch on his way to a feast that was being given in his honour by a master smith called Culan. Watching the strange lopsided game and impressed by the lone boy's strength and skill, Conor invited him to join his company. Setanta answered that he would be glad to follow the king just as soon as the game was over.

Once all the warriors were gathered in Culan's hall, the smith sought the king's leave to set loose his watchdog. It was a massive, terrifying beast, strong as a hundred lesser hounds and more ferocious. Forgetting that he had asked the boy to follow him, Conor granted his permission. So the dog was freed from its chains and muzzle and let out of the door. A few moments later its watchful eyes saw Setanta coming towards the hall. Snarling, with great loping strides, it threw all its vicious bulk at the boy.

Nimble as thought, Setanta hurled his ball into that slavering mouth, jamming its jaws together. Then he seized the dog by its hind legs and, wielding its massive body like a whip, smashed its head against a rock till he had beaten out its brains.

The whole company was drawn out of the hall by the hideous sounds of the struggle. Culan the Smith was furious at the death of his hound and sorely aggrieved by it too, for there was no finer watchdog in all Ireland than that animal had been. Anxious to make amends, the spirited boy responded to his complaints by saying he would make it his business to have another hound found for the smith as good as the one he had killed and to train it up to be as fierce a watchdog. Furthermore, until such a beast was found and trained he would stand guard over Culan's house himself.

'I shall be Culan's hound,' he declared; and when the great druid Cathbad heard those words spoken in the Irish tongue, he foretold that a time would shortly come when that name – Cuchullain, the hound of Culan – would be on the lips of every man.

Not long afterwards it chanced that the boy Cuchullain was eavesdropping as Cathbad the druid gave instruction on the art of divination to his young novices.

One of the pupils asked what were the auguries for that particular day, and Cuchullain heard the druid answer that any man who took arms that day would certainly win a name that outshone any other, but his glorious life would also be cut short.

In those prophetic words Cuchullain heard the sound of his own destiny. Immediately he presented himself before the king, demanding that he be given arms and a chariot as a member of the Red Branch that very day.

Conor stared in wonder and amusement at the mightily precocious seven-year-old. 'Now who would be putting such a powerful thought into your mind?' he asked, smiling.

'None other than your own chief druid Cathbad,' Cuchullain answered.

Taken aback by the confident answer, Conor granted the boy the arms he craved, though it proved a difficult business finding any strong enough for him to wield. Then a charioteer was put at the boy's service and, proudly bearing his newly won arms, Cuchullain drove out into the field.

Hearing the din of the youth's departure, Cathbad came to the king anxiously asking why he had given him arms.

'Was it not on your own advice I did so?' said Conor; but Cathbad denied all knowledge of it, saying that nothing could have been further from his mind and desire than an action which would certainly shorten the life of one so loved.

Yet when Cuchullain returned that night the sides of his chariot were graced with the bloody heads of three warriors whose powerful magical protection had allowed them to take the lives of many brave Ulstermen. By that time the youth was in the first full frenzy of his battle ardour. Throwing out arrogant challenges, he drove his chariot about Emain Macha in such a firebrand state of elation that he was a danger to all. Finally a crowd of naked women went out to distract the boy and calm him down. Amazed by the sight, Cuchullain turned his burning face away. The women caught him in their arms and quickly plunged him into a vat of cold water but his body was so hot that the tub immediately burst its iron hoops apart. When they plunged him into a second vat its water started to boil, and even a third steamed for a long time before the youth at last cooled down.

After that Cuchullain always sat in the place of honour between the feet of the king, and such was his prowess in combat that he soon became the favourite of all the women in Ulster. Yet there was only one of them who commanded the attention of his heart. She was Emer, daughter of Forgal the Wily.

It is said that Emer was the first of all the women in Ireland for the possession of the six gifts: the gift of beauty, the gifts of sonorous voice and gracious speech, the gifts of fine needlework, honour, and wisdom. So when the men of the Red Branch grew envious of the way their women favoured Cuchullain and demanded that a wife quickly be found for him, the young warrior set out to woo Emer for his bride.

Now Forgal was a dangerous man, nephew to a king of the Fomors, and to come safely to his dun was no easy thing. Yet Cuchullain came there and on his arrival Emer recognized him at once as the youth about whom she had already heard much.

'May your path be smooth before you,' she greeted him.

'And may you be safe from all harm,' he replied.

Then, as if she knew nothing either of him or his intentions, Emer asked who he was, and where he had come from; and when Cuchullain had proudly proclaimed his name and lineage, he ventured to ask Emer about herself.

'I am a Tara among women,' she answered proudly. 'One who is gazed at but does not gaze back. I am the reed which is out of reach, the path whose turnings no man has explored. I was brought up in all the ancient virtues and have been often told that I am one on whom all the graces of Ireland's women have been conferred.'

Undaunted by her haughty words, Cuchullain was rather encouraged by them to brag of his own prowess, which he proceeded to do at some length. Emer listened with no visible signs of awe as he told how at his weakest he was stronger than twenty men, and was happy to fight alone against forty, while as many as a hundred might safely shelter under his protection.

'These claims are impressive,' Emer said, ' – for a mere boy. But they are not yet the feats of a true man.' Glancing away from his disappointed frown, she added, 'I have a foster sister whose heart might be moved by them.'

Cuchullain insisted that it was not her sister he desired but Emer herself. Gazing in wonder at the soft flesh between the torque she wore and the cleft of her bosom, he said, 'Fair is that plain of the noble yoke.'

'Yet no one comes to that plain,' Emer answered, 'unless he has leapt the hero's salmon leap, carried off two women with their weight in gold and silver, and three times slain nine men at a single blow, save only that out of each nine a single one be left alive. It is not words alone that will win me, Culan's Hound. I will marry none but one whose name is spoken wherever tales are told of heroes.'

'That fame I would have achieved anyway,' Cuchullain said.

'Then if you can do all that,' Emer said with a sudden relenting softness in her voice, 'your offer is accepted by me, it is taken, it is granted.'

When word of this unsought conditional betrothal found its way to the ears of Forgal, Emer's father thought up a crafty way to rid himself of the danger he foresaw. On a visit to Conor's court he pretended never to have heard of Cuchullain, and having watched some of the young man's feats of arms, was loudly heard to aver that if only such a promising lad dared go to the island of the warlike Queen Scathach in the west of Alba, he might learn such arts of battle there as none might stand against him.

Now it was known that it was hard to reach Scathach's island, and harder still to return, for that fierce queen spared the lives of precious few who came there; but Cuchullain recognized a challenge when he heard one and swore he would do as Forgal had dared.

Two companions set out on the expedition with him but they were soon daunted by the gruelling hardships of the way. When they turned back, Cuchullain pushed on alone, traversing the wild country known as the Plain of Ill-Fortune. Alone he fought his way past the savage beasts in the highland glens, till he came eventually to a wide and sheer gorge that could be crossed only at a single, perilous bridge. The Bridge of the Cliff had been made under a cunning enchantment. As soon as a foot was put on its stones, it would swing straight upwards into the air from the place where it was hinged at the far side, and stand tall as a ship's mast above the gap it left beneath. Three times Cuchullain tried to make the crossing and three times he failed as the bridge reared up before him. Then his heart grew thunderous with anger, the hot light of his frenzy glowed about his head, and driven on by the power of his rage, he approached the bridge at a run, leaping like a salmon from the ground, without touching the stones. That single bound took him high in the air and down onto the middle of the bridge. As soon as he landed, the bridge began to lift, but from that central place he could slide down easily to the other side.

When he came at last to Scathach's dun on the Isle of Mists, Cuchullain took the fierce queen by surprise. Holding his naked sword at her breast, he threatened to kill her before the eyes of her two sons if she did not take him into her tribe and teach him all she knew about the arts of war. Impressed by the youth's fearlessness, and preferring life over needless death, Scathach agreed to put him through her initiations.

During his time among her people, Cuchullain became skilled in all the subtler arts of war. It was there that he befriended an Irish youth called Ferdiad who was himself a warrior of formidable powers, and deep bonds of love and loyalty grew between them. Those bonds were sealed with oaths of lifelong friendship.

When war broke out between Scathach and Aife, who was renowned as the most savage female warrior in the world, it was Cuchullain who finally overcame the fearsome woman. He forced her to render up hostages to Scathach, and some say that at that time both Aife and Scathach herself gave Culan's Hound the friendship of their loins.

Yet Cuchullain's heart lay in Ireland still, and with his own fierce strength now finely tuned to Scathach's knowledge, he returned to Forgal's dun in his scythed chariot, loudly demanding the hand of the chieftain's daughter, Emer.

Forgal sent three groups of nine warriors out against him, but each time Cuchullain slew eight of them with a single blow. From each of the bands he spared only Scibur, Ibur and Cat, who were Emer's brothers. Forgal himself fled in terror at the approach of this terrifying contender for his daughter's hand, and in the panic of his haste he fell from his own rampart, killing himself in the fall. So Cuchullain carried off both Emer and her foster sister, together with their weight in gold and silver, thus meeting the last of the conditions that Emer had laid on him.

So great was the fame that came to him by these deeds that at every feast at Conor's court in Emain Macha it was Cuchullain and his fair wife Emer who took precedence over all the rest of that proud host.

Now at the time Conor mac Nessa was king in Ulster, and the land of Connaught was ruled by Queen Maeve and her husband King Ailill. A passionate rivalry raged between that queen and her husband, and in no matter were they more contentious than in jealous pride over their possessions. One day, caught in a violent row about which of them was the richer, they began counting out their treasures. They found that in the count of coin and jewels, of clothing and fine linen, of precious vessels and household goods, of flocks of sheep, and herds of horses, and droves of swine, there was not a jot to choose between their two vast hoards of wealth.

Only in a single matter was an imbalance found: among King Ailill's cattle herd was a marvellous bull called the White-horned One, and for that majestic creature the furious Queen Maeve possessed no match.

Now though Ailill's bull was one of a pair, there was a reason for this discrepancy. In another incarnation, both bulls had been swineherds, one to the King of Munster, the other to the King of Connaught, and the two had been jealous rivals over the merits of their herds. They were often enough in the way of quarrelling and fighting, and the better to fight out their quarrels, they were in the habit of changing shape. For one struggle they transformed themselves into ravens, for another into water-monsters. Once they fought as great human champions and, on the last fateful occasion, they changed themselves into eels. Now when they were in the form of eels, one of the two swam into a river in that part of Ulster known as Cuailgne, and there it was swallowed up by a cow belonging to a chief called Daire. At the same time the other eel swam into a spring in Connaught where it too was swallowed by a drinking cow, and that animal belonged among the herd of Queen Maeve.

Out of those two cows were born a famous pair of prize bulls that were brawnier, and nobler of haunch and horn, than any two bulls that had been seen before. They were known as the

White-Horned One of Connaught and the Brown Bull of Cuailgne; and all might have been well except that the white bull thought it base scorn to belong among the cattle of a woman, so he deserted Maeve's herd for that of her husband Ailill.

Enraged to the point of madness now to find herself poorer than her husband to the tune of a single bull that had once been rightfully hers, Maeve was determined to square accounts again. The quickest way about it was to send ambassadors with gifts to Cuailnge, asking Daire if he would not let her have the loan of his Brown Bull for the space of a single year.

Being a generous-hearted man, Daire was willing enough to respond to her request and would have gladly done so, but one of the ambassadors from Connaught took too much ale at the feasting that night and was heard to boast that, had the bull not been freely lent, Maeve would have taken it anyway by force. When word of this arrogance reached Daire, he angrily withdrew his consent, and the ambassadors were packed off back to Connaught without the bull craved by their Queen.

Outraged at this refusal, Maeve summoned the fighting men of Ireland to join her in a cattle-raid on Cuailnge. Now Fergus son of Roy, the exiled Ulsterman, was in Connaught at that time. He had once been foster father to Cuchullain and one of Ulster's greatest champions, but he had abandoned his homeland after Conor's treachery in the matter of Deirdre and Naoise had left both the sons of Fergus dead. The embittered champion gladly rallied to Maeve's cause, and she put that peerless warrior at the head of her troops.

There were reasons why she felt sure they must enjoy an easy victory. Many years before that time an ancestor of Conor mac Nessa had fallen foul of the powerful goddess Macha, who was wife to Nuada of the Silver Hand. In retaliation for an insult, Macha had laid a hereditary curse on the fighting men of Ulster that in times of trouble they must endure for a time all the weakness suffered by women in childbirth. Sure that this affliction must now fall on the warriors of the Red Branch, Maeve called out one of her wise women to prophesy her victory.

'How do you see our hosts?' she asked the seer.

'I see them all covered in crimson,' the sibyl replied.

'That cannot be. Surely the warriors of Ulster are all enfeebled by their curse,' cried Maeve. 'Look again. Tell me how you see our hosts.'

'I see them covered in crimson' the sibyl said again, 'I see them all red.' Then, in the wild possession of her trance, she went on to tell the bewildered queen how she saw a young man single-handedly performing wondrous deeds of valour. 'There are many wounds on his skin,' she said, 'but the light of victory glows about his head. I see all our army reddened at his hand. The slaughter he makes will not soon be forgotten. Our women will howl over the bodies mangled by this Hound of the Forge.'

And this was the way it was to fall out, for Cuchullain's true father, Lugh, was no Ulsterman but one among the Everliving Ones, so the youth was not subject to the curse that laid the rest of the Red Branch low. Moreover Fergus had secretly sent word to him of the coming raid on Ulster, for though Cuchullain's foster father had no love for Conor mac Nessa, he could not bring himself to lead an attack on his ailing countrymen without giving fair warning. So, as Maeve's great army launched its assault on Cuailnge, its fighting men found Cuchullain and his chariot-driver standing in their way.

Swiftly he cut down each champion that tried to remove him. Warrior after warrior fell at his feet. Then, when challengers were slower to come, he harassed the army with his slingshot, felling a hundred fighting men or more each day. Soon the people in Maeve's camp dared scarcely move for fear of his missiles. The queen's lapdog dropped dead under one of his stones, then her pet bird and her squirrel were killed. Even Maeve herself escaped death only narrowly when one of her attendants tried on her golden head-dress, only to have a pebble burst through her skull into the brain beneath.

Astonished that a single man could keep an entire army pinned down this way, the passionate queen determined to see this hero for herself. A herald was sent out demanding parley, and when Cuchullain stepped forth to talk, Maeve was amazed to find herself confronting a youth barely seventeen years old.

Using all her wiles, she offered him her friendship, promising him the reward of great possessions in Connaught if he would abandon the cause of the Ulstermen and put his strength in her own service. But plead as she might, all her promises and blandishments were rejected. Again and again she sent heralds out with ever more prodigal inducements, and each time the hero was unmoved. Finally he grew so impatient with their futile entreaties that he swore to cut the head off the next man who troubled him that way.

Yet Culan's Hound was growing weary of inaction and there was one bargain he was prepared to strike.

He declared that if a single champion dared to come out against him each day, then he would allow the main army to advance towards Cuailnge for just so long as the combat lasted. But as soon as their champion had fallen, the entire host of Connaught must come to a halt again until a new challenger came forth the following day.

Seeing she could hope for no better bargain, Maeve accepted these terms. Each morning she offered the hand of her daughter to any man who could bring her Cuchullain's head; but as each fresh contender was enticed, the army had time to advance no more than a few yards before the fight ended and the man's name was added to the growing list of the dead. Warrior after warrior was toppled from his chariot or fell at the Ulsterman's feet. But while Cuchullain was thus tied down by daily challenges, Maeve sent out scouts to search the meadows of Ulster for the Brown Bull, the desire for which noble beast had already cost her so much. Found at last, the bull was driven back steaming into Maeve's camp along with fifty heifers that had followed him out of Daire's herd. Yet Maeve's brief triumph proved a bitter one. Humiliated at being promised to a different man each day, her daughter died from the shame of it.

Meanwhile Cuchullain's exploits had not gone unwatched by the Everliving Ones who preside over the destinies of men. As the hero slept one night he was wakened by a terrible, summoning shout that came out of the north.

Leaping into his chariot, he hastened northwards till he came to a place where he found a tall woman waiting for him in a crimson war-chariot that was drawn by a roan-red horse. The woman was dressed all in red, with a long red cloak clasped over her red gown, and against the pale glamour of her face even her eyebrows were a fiery red, though in her hand she held a long grey spear.

When Cuchullain demanded to know who she was, the woman declared herself to be the proud daughter of a great king, one who had heard much of Cuchullain's exploits. And the more she had heard of them, she said, the more fiercely had her heart burned for the love of him and for the desire of his company.

'Then if you are alert to my deeds,' Cuchullain answered, 'you will know I have more pressing things on my mind than love.'

Silenced for a moment by this unexpected rebuff, the woman studied Cuchullain keenly. 'And if you are alert to what is happening around you,' she said, 'you will know that I have been giving you my help in every fight, and may continue to do so still.'

'Cuchullain needs no woman's help,' the hero snorted.

'Take back that word,' the woman said, and when Cuchullain would not take it back, the offended queen turned a gaze of flame upon him. 'Then if you will not have my help,' she said, 'you shall have my hatred and my enmity instead. Soon you will face a warrior that is more of a match for you, and you will see how I come against you then to give him the advantage.'

At that Cuchullain drew his sword, but in the same instant woman and chariot disappeared, and all he saw in the dusky air about him was the shadow of a hoodie crow upon a branch.

Then, for the first time, the heart of Cuchullain quailed, for he knew that the face of the Morrigan herself was set against him.

Though Maeve now had the Brown Bull in her possession, she too was filled with fury by the disdain with which Cuchullain had rejected her advances. The next day she sent out the veteran Loch against him, and when Loch swore he would not fight with a beardless youth, Cuchullain stained his chin with blackberry juice to make it seem all grizzled. Stung by such contempt, Loch threw himself against the youth while, unknown to him, the Morrigan worked her magic at the challenger's side.

Three times she came against Cuchullain – firstly as a crazy heifer that sought to gore him on its horns; then as an eel that almost made him fall as it slid under his feet when the two warriors struggled in the river; and lastly as a wolf which gripped his right arm in its vicious jaws. Cuchullain fought off each of these attacks by breaking the heifer's leg, trampling on the eel, and putting out the wolf's eye; but Loch took full advantage of their help to thrust his own blows home.

At last Cuchullain saw that he would win this struggle only by resorting to his many-barbed spear, the *Gae Bolga*, which gave him an invincible advantage over all contenders. So with a heavy heart he used it and the fight was hideously over.

But Cuchullain had taken so many grievous wounds in the bitter struggle that the gods took pity on him as he limped away to bathe them.

It is said that even the Morrigan herself was seen to come to him in the guise of an old woman tending the wounds he had taken at her hand, for they were of the kind that could be healed only by the one who dealt them. Cuchullain's true father, Lugh the Longhanded, also visited him in the guise of a handsome stranger, dressed in green and gold, who gave him a draught that made the hero sleep for three days and nights. And as Cuchullain slept, Lugh lay powerful herbs on his many wounds so that when the warrior woke again he was fresh and vigorous as on the first day of battle.

It is also said that a company of boys who had been close companions to Cuchullain once, came out of Emain Macha to fight in his place while he slept, and though they killed three times their own number among Maeve's men, every one of them was slain.

The time had now come when Maeve demanded that Fergus himself must go out and fight against Cuchullain; but that noble-hearted man immediately refused to lift his weapons against the youth he had fostered and loved as he watched him grow up in Emain Macha. Only when Maeve taunted him with cowardice before the host did he agree to meet his foster son in battle, and he refused to take with him the famous sword of his protection.

Cuchullain's heart ached when he saw his own foster father coming against him, but Fergus was no friend to Ulster now and so he lifted his own weapons to meet him. Then he noticed that Fergus was not carrying the sword on which his life depended.

'Go back, foster father,' he shouted. 'It is foolishness to come against me without your sword.'

'Even if I were carrying my sword,' Fergus answered, 'I would not lift it against you.'

'You have always been dear to me, Fergus,' Cuchullain cried in bewilderment,' and I know that Conor wronged you. I have no wish to shed your blood, yet if you try to lead Ulster's enemies past me I must surely cut you down.'

'Then you would have the death of your own foster father on your head. Yet I cannot return to Maeve without raising my arm against you.'

'Then there is a destiny on us,' said Cuchullain sadly.

'Perhaps it is not the one you think,' Fergus answered, lowering his voice. 'It is Conor I hate not Ulster, and you are as dear to me as those sons of mine he murdered. I would not have him come between us now. For the sake of all that was between us once, I entreat you to let us find another way.'

'My sworn loyalty to Conor is as great as your hatred for him,' said Cuchullain. 'What other way can there be?'

'If we were to feign battle for a time and you were seen to turn and flee, then you would be spared the guilt of your foster-father's blood and I could return to Maeve with honour.'

'Dearly as I love you,' Cuchullain answered, 'it would be hard for me to run before any man.'

'And for me also,' said Fergus. 'But if, for the love that is between us, you were to do this thing, then I swear that in a future battle, at a time of your own choosing, I too will throw away my arms and run.' And when Cuchullain still hesitated, he sighed, 'My heart is no longer in this war. I think some great advantage may come to Ulster from this bargain.'

'Do I have your oath on that?' Cuchullain said.

'If you need my oath, you have it.'

So the two champions clashed their weapons for a time until, to the amazement and the loud derision of the men of Connaught, Cuchullain was seen to turn on his heel and run; and when Fergus returned to the camp of that relentless queen, she could find no cause to reproach him.

Yet Cuchullain remained alive, and now Maeve stooped to trickery to bring about his end. Among her forces were Calatin the Enchanter and his twenty-seven sons, all armed with poisoned spears that never missed their mark. Though it had been agreed that only a single challenger should fight with Cuchullain each day, Maeve declared that Calatin and his sons must be considered one, for they were all of the same body.

Fergus was filled with shame and grief when he heard of this deceit. Unwilling to watch Cuchullain's death himself, he despatched a fellow exiled Ulsterman called Fiacha to watch the fight and bring back his report. And when Fiacha saw Cuchullain treacherously assailed by so many at once and almost overwhelmed, his heart went out at the injustice of it. Drawing his sword, he sprang down from the rocks to stand at Cuchullain's side and together they slew Calatin and all his brood.

Now Maeve was left with but a single resort. There was only one champion left among her forces who might stand against the might of Cuchullain – an Irish warrior whose skin was hard as horn so that no ordinary weapon could ever penetrate it. His name was Ferdia.

It was he with whom Cuchullain had been initiated among Scathach's people on the Isle of Mists. It was he with whom Cuchullain had sworn lifelong bonds of love and loyalty; and it was for these reasons that Ferdia had not taken arms against the champion before.

Nor was he willing to do so now, for the love he felt for his friend was far stronger than his allegiance to Maeve.

Seeing that means of inciting the man must be found, Maeve lyingly declared that she had heard Cuchullain boasting that he had no fear of Ferdia and could easily vanquish him. But Ferdia claimed he knew it for a lie; and even if it were true, he would not foreswear his oaths of friendship even though Cuchullain himself had done so.

Maeve declared that this sounded like a coward's answer, and that the only words that were not cheap were those of the satirists among her poets. If Ferdia was afraid to fight for the honour of his name, she said, then she would call upon those bards to lampoon him with such cruel scorn that the otherwise impenetrable skin of his face would break into blisters and he must surely die from the shame of it. Then in sweeter vein, she promised that if Ferdia dared to take the field then she would bind herself with six sureties for the great rewards that would come to him upon his victory.

Eventually, driven by such lies, threats and inducements, Ferdia reluctantly set out against Cuchullain.

When the hero saw his friend approach he joyfully made to greet him, but Ferdia said that he had not come there as a friend. Fate had set its face against their friendship and it was now their time to fight.

Bewildered by the tragic turn his stand was taking, and with the memory of the love and loyalty that had grown between them lively in his breast, Cuchullain begged Ferdia to withdraw. But Ferdia had committed himself too far and, though he too was anguished by emotion, withdrawal was no longer possible. So with heavy hearts the two champions urged their chariots against each other and at the end of a whole day's fighting neither had yielded a single yard of ground. Weary from their exertions, they kissed each other then, and returned to their tents to rest themselves before the fight should be resumed again at dawn. That night Cuchullain sent half of the healing herbs that Lugh had given him to soothe Ferdia's wounds. Their horses were stabled together as in the old days, and their chariot-drivers slept by the same fire.

When the two heroes rose the next day, they fought again from dawn to sunset with neither gaining the advantage. A third day's struggle found no outcome either, but at the end of that day the champions parted gloomily, and now their horses and charioteers were kept apart, for it was sure that one or other of them must fall on the morrow.

On the fourth day Ferdia came out shouting his defiance of Cuchullain. 'I have come as a wild boar of the herd,' he bellowed, 'to thrust you under the waters of the ford. For it is I, Ferdia, who can crush you, and may the death of their champion long be a grievous loss to the men of Emain Macha.'

It is said by some that at this shout two invisible helpers came to aid Cuchullain out of the fairy world, and that when Ferdia noticed their presence, he rancorously accused the Ulsterman of seizing an unfair advantage. Angrily, Cuchullain answered that if such powers had come to his assistance it could only be to compensate for the imbalance caused by Ferdia's own impenetrable skin. So the rage of frustration grew on the two champions as they hacked at each other with neither giving way.

At last, when his invisible protectors were killed, the champion of the Ulstermen let the full frenzy of his battle ardour come upon him. In that terrible condition he reached for his invincible spear, the *Gae Bolga*, which honour had prevented him from using before. Thrusting with all his might he forced it up into Ferdia's body through the one place it might enter. Once inside, that terrible weapon opened up its barbs.

With the battle frenzy passing from him now, Cuchullain found himself watching the friend he had once loved dying in unspeakable agony at his feet. The sight of it filled his heart with an immense grief. Tenderly he bent to pick up the torn body and carried it back across the river to the Ulster side so that Ferdia should not be buried among the warriors of Connaught, but would lie instead among Cuchullain's own kind. And as he wept, a great bewailing cry of lamentation broke from Cuchullain's mouth.

'It was all as a game,' he cried, 'until my friend Ferdia came against me, and now the shadow of his death will hang across me like a cloud for ever.'

After all the long days of struggle Cuchullainn's body was now so covered in wounds that he could no longer bear the touch of his clothes about him. Word of his suffering reached Sualtam, Dechtire's husband, who had accepted the newborn Cuchullain as his own son. 'Is it the sound of heaven breaking that assaults my ears,' cried Sualtam, 'or of the sea pouring away, or of the earth quaking apart; or is it the groaning of my own dear son that I hear?' Then he came where the exhausted hero lay, and when he saw his body blue with bruises and gashed with blood, Sualtam would have fought for vengeance; but Cuchullain bade him rather ride at once to Etain Macha and tell Conor and the warriors of the Red Branch that his strength was almost at an end and he could no longer defend Ulster without their aid.

Mounted on Cuchullain's own great warhorse, the 'Grey of Battle', Sualtam hastened to Conor's fort at Etain Macha where he cried out how men were being slain, and women carried off, and cattle lifted in Ulster. Cathbad the Druid was the first to rise from the curse of infirmity, berating this loud intruder for disturbing his rest. Sualtam turned his mount away from the insult so furiously that the Grey of Battle reared back, forcing the sharp edge of his rider's shield against his neck with a violence that took Sualtam's head clean off. Yet so urgent was the rage that was on him that, as it rolled on the ground, his severed head continued to shout out its warning: 'To arms! To arms! Men are being slain, and women carried off, and cattle lifted in Ulster.'

The strangeness of the omen was enough to rouse all the men of the Red Branch from their enfeeblement. When they had gathered their strength again, Conor swore a great oath of vengeance before them. 'The sky is above us,' he vowed, 'and the earth beneath, and the wide sea circles all around us; and unless the stars fall, or the earth collapse, or the seas come to cover all the land, then I shall return every beast to its pasture and every woman to her home.'

Heralds were sent across Ulster to rally all the fighting men. Rapidly they came to the place where Maeve's host had been halted by the champion, and there the two armies clashed together.

When Cuchullain heard the din of fighting round him, he forgot his wounds and picked up his weapons again. Advancing on the foe, he saw Fergus fighting in the front rank of the Connaught men.

'Remember our bargain, foster father,' Cuchullain shouted. Hearing his words, Fergus threw down the weight of his weapons and, turning on his heel before Cuchullain, ran away. When Maeve's fighting men saw their leader take so shamelessly to flight, the heart went out of them. Their line wavered and broke till all Maeve's army fled in panicked rout before the triumphant push of the Ulstermen.

Yet the first cause of all this bloody conflict, the great Brown Bull of Cuailnge, was still held captive by Maeve's herdsmen. They drove the animal back to their queen's pastures in Connaught, but even there Maeve was to find no lasting satisfaction, for when the Brown Bull of Cuailnge came up against the White-Horned One that belonged to King Ailill, there was instant hatred between them.

Lowering its horns, the Brown Bull thrust its massive weight against its white rival, and a tremendous battle began between the two beasts in which they rampaged over all the green fields of Ireland, bellowing in their steam as they fought. At last the Brown Bull was seen at Cruachan, the high seat of Connacht, with the white limbs of its opponent hanging in bloody pieces from its horns. Then, with a great moan, the Brown Bull turned its battered head away from Connaught and went back to its own pastures in Cuailnge.

So the accounts between Maeve and Ailill were now balanced again, for both of them had suffered great losses in that war and neither of them now possessed a bull of such great price. But the ferocity of its long fight had crazed the mind of the Brown Bull of Cuailnge, and when it found its way home again it was a danger to all who came near. Not long afterwards, its fierce heart burst from all its mad bellowing and the bull fell down stone dead. In that way came an end to the great war that was ever afterwards called the Cattle Raid of Cuailnge.

There were many other marvels and adventures in Cuchullain's short but glorious life, for Queen Maeve never forgave the defeat she had suffered at his hands, nor did she tire of rousing enemies against him. Proudest among these were the Kings of Munster and Leinster, both of whom he slew; but his most dangerous foes were the daughters of Calatin the Enchanter, who had been born after the wizard's death and sent to the Isle of Alba to learn the powers of witchcraft there. On their return to Ireland they worked many enchantments on Cuchullain, by which they sought to draw him out to where he might be slain. But Cuchullain was under the protection of Cathbad the Druid, and the three witches had no joy of their sorcery until their magical powers at last made the hero believe that the whole province of Ulster was ravaged and put to flame.

At once Cuchullain set out against his illusory foes though every omen warned against the adventure. His horse, the Grey of Battle, refused its bridle and was seen to shed tears of blood. When his mother, Dechtire, brought him a goblet of wine where he stood in his chariot beside Laig, his charioteer, the wine turned to blood at his lips. More dreadful still, at the first ford he crossed he saw a maiden washing out blood-stained battle garments which she said were the clothes of Cuchullain who must shortly die.

But Cuchullain drove on after his fate undaunted, till his chariot came to a place where three hags huddled round a fire at the roadside, each of them blinded in the left eye. There were spits made of rowan wood set up over that fire and the hags were roasting the flesh of a dog across its heat. One of them smiled up at Cuchullain as his chariot approached, and bade him come share their meal with them.

Now all his life Cuchullain had lived under the prohibition that he would eat no dog meat, for he was himself the Hound of Culan, and would not eat the flesh of the animal whose name he had taken for his own. So he refused the offer and would have bidden Laig drive on; but the hag that had asked him claimed that he refused her only because he was too proud to be seen eating their humble fare.

'If we were rich like your friends,' she jeered at him, 'you would have joined us eagerly enough.'

Stung by this remark, Cuchullain declared it was no great shame for him to eat with the poor, so he stood down from his chariot and sat with them on the ground. Smiling, the hag tore the shoulderblade from the dog's roasted carcass, and Cuchullain took it from her hand. As the hags watched him, the hero did no more than pretend to gnaw the bone before deftly hiding it away beneath his thigh. Yet even so he felt a great part of his strength drain from the hand which had touched the meat and from the thigh which concealed it.

In that instant he saw that it was Calatin's daughters who had injured him so. Leaping to his feet he saw a troop of his greatest enemies coming up against him. At their head was Lughaidh, son of that King of Munster whom Cuchullain had killed, and his ally Erc, whose father, the King of Leinster, had also fallen at Cuchullain's hands. Feeling the want of the strength that had gone from him, the Ulsterman looked urgently to his defence.

Now on that day Cuchullain was armed with the three spears of which it was said that each was destined to kill a king. His enemies must have known of this, for among their company were three bards, and it is an unlucky thing for a man to refuse whatever a bard might ask of him.

'Give me one of those spears in your chariot,' demanded the first bard, 'or I will make such a satire on your name as will shame it for ever.'

'Take it,' said Cuchullain, 'for never shall I be shamed for refusing a bard.'

And he threw the spear, killing the bard instantly. But Lughaidh, the young King of Munster, pulled out the spear and hurled it back, killing Laig with it, who was the king among chariot drivers.

Then a second bard demanded a spear of Cuchullain, threatening to lampoon the entire province of Ulster if he was refused.

'I am not obliged to give more than once in a day,' the hero answered, 'but none shall shame Ulster because of me,' and he threw the spear so that it went straight through the head of the bard. But Erc, the King of Leinster, caught it as it fell, and threw it back in vengeance for his dead father. That spear pierced the side of the Grey of Battle, which was the king of all warhorses. With a heart-rending cry, Cuchullain's horse broke free of his yoke and staggered into the shallows of a nearby pool, leaving his master with only a single horse harnessed to his chariot.

Then the third bard demanded the last spear of Cuchullain.

'Have I not sorely paid for all that is due both from me and Ulster?' Cuchullain demanded.

'Refuse me,' answered the bard, 'and my satire shall bring scorn on all your kindred.'

'I think I shall never see my home again,' Cuchullain shouted, 'yet my race shall not bear scorn because of me.' Then he hurled his last spear, instantly felling the bard. Again Lughaidh drew out the spear and hurled it back whence it had come, and this was the spear that mortally pierced the belly of the man who was a king among warriors. Knowing that his death was on him, Cuchullain pulled out the spear and with his hands holding the burst entrails at his stomach, asked his foes to let him go to the water to drink.

They watched in awe-stricken silence as he staggered towards the pool with the strength fading swiftly from his limbs. When Cuchullain found he could walk no further, he leaned against a standing-stone that was in that place, and bound himself to it with his harness so that he might at least die on his feet. As Lughaid and Erc closed in on him with their followers, the Grey of Battle found a last surge of strength and reared his flashing hooves in defence of his master, killing more of his foes before falling dead to the ground.

But the hero-light was already growing dim about Cuchullain's head, and the face that had once burned ruddy with his battle ardour was now pale as the snow of a single night. It was then, as the last life went out of the champion where he stood, strapped upright to the stone, that a hoodie crow flapped out of the gloom to perch at his shoulder. The Morrigan had come at last to claim Cuchullain for her own.

Seeing this, his foes were sure that the life was gone out of him. It was Lughaidh who hacked off Cuchullain's noble head that Queen Maeve might have it in her sight. Yet even in death the warrior fought on, for as his grip loosened and his great sword fell, the blade severed Lughaid's hand at the wrist.

It is said that they cut off Cuchullain's lifeless right hand in revenge. Yet none lived long to enjoy this triumph over the greatest of all fighting men, for his friend Conall the Victorious soon brought up the Red Branch in pursuit of Ulster's foes, and wrought great havoc among them there. It was Conall who took vengeance on Lughaidh, King of Munster, fighting him with one of his own hands fastened at his back out of fairness to the maimed man, yet still managing to slice off Lughaidh's head.

Such was the manner of the death of Ulster's greatest champion in the twenty-seventh year of his young life; and the Red Branch of Ulster would never again know such glory as came to its name in Cuchullain's day.

4

The Pursuit of Diarmaid and Grainne

In the days when Cormac mac Art ruled over Ireland from his seat at Tara of the Kings, there was a proud war band called the Fianna and their chief was Finn mac Cool. Now it was the sworn duty of the Fianna to guard the coasts of Ireland and come to the aid of any prince of the isle whose lands were invaded by foreign foes; and it was no easy thing to become a member of that band.

A fighting man of the Fianna was not only a fierce warrior but a poet and a man of fine culture too, and one who had put himself under many hard oaths. Thus he must renounce all revenge on his family's behalf and never seek vengeance from them either. He must vow never to turn his back on the enemy in battle, never to refuse hospitality to any who asked it of him, never to give offence to womankind, and to demand no dowry when he took himself a wife. Nor was that the end of it, for there were many ordeals he must endure to prove himself worthy of admission to the band. Only a man who could stand waist deep in a pit, armed with nothing more than shield and hazel wand to fend off the spears of nine warriors hurled all at once without taking injury, might join their number. Then, given no more than a tree-length's start, he must run the thickness of a wood and if any of the armed men giving chase put so much as a scratch on him he could not join the band. Nor could he do so if he tangled his hair in the chase or broke a branch from a tree, or if any saw his spear shake in his hand when the chase was done. Moreover the bodily prowess of these men was a wonder to observe, for it is said they could pluck thorns from their heels while running at full pelt, leaping over high branches and bending under boughs as low as their knees.

So they were brave and cultivated men, the warriors of the Fianna, and none more so than their leader Finn mac Cool, who if not the strongest of their number, was certainly the truest, the wisest and most open-handed. For it was said of Finn that if the dead trash of leaves in the forest was all gold, and the white foam on the waters silver, he would gladly have given it all away.

There was a great marvel that lay at the root of Finn's wisdom, and it came from the time when he was raised as a youth in the mountains of Slieve Bloom. The boy's father had been killed before his birth in a bitter battle between two rival clans. Finn's own people were scattered in that war and he was raised by his mother secretly in the wild so that their enemies should not find and kill him. The youth, who was called Deimne at that time, became a fine athlete and hunter, whom all thought fair to look upon. He came one day to the banks of the Boyne where he was taken as servant by a reclusive man of knowledge called Finn the Seer. For the length of seven years that hermit had been waiting to catch the

Salmon of Knowledge in the deep pool near Slane because it had been foretold that the salmon would yield up its gift of universal wisdom to a man called Finn when he caught and ate it.

Shortly after Deimne came to him, the hermit caught the salmon and gave it to his servant to cook, warning him to eat no morsel of its flesh. But sensing a strangeness about the youth when he returned with the cooked fish the Seer asked if he had eaten any part of it. 'I did not,' Deimne replied, 'but as I turned the salmon I burned my thumb and a blister rose there, so I put it to my mouth to ease the pain of it.'

'You told me your name was Deimne,' said his master in sudden, dreadful suspicion. 'Do you have any other name?'

'I do,' the youth answered, and it was true because as he had grown towards manhood so many people had asked to know who that 'fair' one was that he had been given the word for his second name. 'The name I have taken,' he said, 'is Deimne Finn.'

'Then it was for you this salmon was destined,' said Finn the Seer sadly. 'Now you must eat it all.'

When the young Finn did as he was bidden the gift of wisdom came on him. In later life, whenever he stood in need of counsel he need only suck on his thumb of knowledge and he would know at once all things that he needed to know.

The story goes on to tell how Finn wisely used his magical gift to confound his father's enemies and persuade them to join with his own people so that the two clans became one, the Fianna, over which Finn wisely ruled. As his powers grew, this most just and gifted of men took tribute from all the Kings of Ireland and put his independent strength at their service in many brave and marvellous exploits. It was the Fianna who rid their lands of every kind of giant, dragon and monster that came to trouble them. Yet if Finn was a seer and a poet and a mighty warrior, perhaps his greatest joy lay in the hunt.

The Fianna were all fine hunting men and many of their greatest adventures began with a chase through the forest that would lead them into magical enchantments and end in bloodshed. Yet because of their truthfulness and the power of their hands, they emerged victorious from all such dangers.

Finn himself had two fine hunting hounds, Bran and Sceolan, who were magical creatures, close as kin to him, and were in fact his own nephews born of Finn's sister when she was transformed into a bitch by sorcery. Finn's love of the hunt was reflected in the names given to his son, Oisin, which means 'a fawn', and to his grandson, Oscar, which means 'one who loves the deer.'

By following an enchanted fawn into the forest, Finn, Oisin and Oscar were drawn into an alliance with the fairy gods of the *sidh* against a great host that had come to attack them; and the tale of The Chase of the Enchanted Pigs of Aengus tells how a heated rivalry between Finn and the god Aengus, as to whether Finn's hounds were stronger than the god's swine, might have led to a disastrous war between gods and heroes had not Finn wisely decided to opt for peace.

Yet the most powerful tale of Finn as a hunting-man tells not about the enchanted chasing after a deer or a boar, but of the doom laden pursuit of a woman and the man she loved, and this is the way of that sad story.

It was in the time when the years were making an old man of Finn, and good sleep had not come to him often since the death of his wife. Longing for a companion in his old age, he sent word to Cormac mac Art, the High King at Tara, that he wished to wed his daughter, Grainne. Now there could be no nobler match for a king's daughter than to be wedded to Finn, the hero of all Ireland, but things had not always been easy between Cormac and Finn, and Grainne was known to have refused the hand of every man that asked for it. So it was a matter of relief to all, that when Cormac asked Grainne whether she would consent to the wedding, she answered that if Finn was a fitting son-in-law for her father, then why should he not be a fitting husband for her.

So Finn was invited to claim his bride at a great wedding feast to be held at the king's high seat. Accompanied by his chosen men, Finn came to Tara in great state and was warmly welcomed by Cormac the King. Yet Grainne herself took less pleasure in Finn's arrival, for though she had heard much of his great deeds, and her passionate heart had quickened at those tales, she had never set eyes on Finn before. She was dismayed now to find that the man to whom she was betrothed was already older than her own father.

'It is a great wonder, that Finn did not seek me out in marriage for his son, Oisin, rather than for himself,' she thought, 'for the match would have been more fitting.' Yet Finn found Grainne as fair as he had dreamed, and as they sat together he sought to charm his betrothed by letting her display her powers of quick speech in answer to his riddles.

'What is whiter than the snow?' he asked.

'The truth,' she said at once.

'And what is sharper than a sword?'

'The wit of a woman between two men.'

'And what is quicker than the wind?' asked Finn.

'A woman's mind,' Grainne answered, and in all her answers she uttered no word of a lie; but the truth was, she had no love for Finn; and at the wedding feast as the food was served, and the songs were sung, and all the noble company made good cheer, her eager eyes were everywhere but on the man to whom she was betrothed.

Finn's druid sat beside her at the table, and Grainne asked him the names of all the company who had accompanied Finn to the feast. One by one the druid named the heroes of the Fianna until lastly she asked, 'And who is that fair-speaking man who sits at Oisin's left hand?'

'That is Diarmaid, son of Duibhne,' the druid answered, 'third man of the Fianna, after only Finn himself and Finn's son Oisin, and the best lover of women in the wide world.'

And while Grainne gazed on the handsome face of that dark haired man who wore a cap dashingly pulled down across his brow, there was a loud commotion among the dogs fighting for scraps beneath the table. As Diarmaid rose to part them, the cap covering part of his temple fell from his head, and at the sight of the love-spot suddenly revealed there, Grainne felt her heart ravished by ungovernable love for the man.

With flame rising at her throat, she called to her serving-maid, telling her to bring from the sun-room the great golden drinking cup that would hold wine enough for almost all that company. When the cup was brought, Grainne secretly drugged the wine that was in it, and with her own hand carried it to Finn, bidding him drink deep. Then she passed on round the tables so that no man could refuse her until the cup was empty, and all had drunk from it except Diarmaid himself along with Finn's son, Oisin, his grandson Oscar, and the Druid who sat at Grainne's side.

It was not long before all who had drunk from the cup fell into deep slumber. Then Grainne rose from her place and with the breath taut at her throat stood before Diarmaid, saying, 'I am asking that you take my love, Diarmaid, son of Duibhne, and that you bring me out of this house tonight.'

Astonished by her words, Diarmaid swore that he would have no secret dealings with a woman who was already promised to his lord. 'It is a great wonder that you give your love to me, daughter of Cormac, and not to Finn,' he protested, 'for there is no greater lover of woman in the land than he.'

Then Grainne told the bewildered man how she had been gazing on his face when the cap fell from his brow, revealing the love-spot there, and how her heart had instantly filled with a love so powerful that she could not live long if it remained unanswered.

Now Diarmaid knew the power of the love-spot that had been put on his brow by the god Aengus, and it was for that very reason he had striven to keep it concealed. Lamenting the unhappy chance that had let Grainne's gaze fall on it, he strove now to resist the claims of her love, saying that even if he wished to betray his loyalty to Finn, he dare not do it.

'Yet is it not said of the Fianna both that they are fearless and that they must never give offence to womankind?' said Grainne.

'It is,' Diarmaid admitted.

'Then do I put you under bonds not to refuse me now,' she cried, and saw Diarmaid blanch at the conflict opened in his mind by the power of her invocation. 'I shall wait for you by the walls of Tara,' she said, leaving him then, 'and if you are a true man you will carry me away from this place tonight before Finn and the King my father wake from their sleep.'

Trapped between loyalty to his lord and a bond that no man could honourably break, Diarmaid turned in hot confusion of mind to those of his friends who were still awake, telling them what had happened and asking their advice.

'Though I am my father's son,' Oisin answered, 'I tell you that if the woman has laid her bonds on you, no guilt can fall to you in going with her.' And Oscar, Finn's grandson, added further that there could be no greater shame for a man than to break the sacred bonds laid on him by a woman.

Still agonized by the conflict, Diarmaid turned at last to Finn's druid for his counsel. Shaking his head, the druid answered, 'I too tell you to go with Grainne, though it is in my mind that you will get your death by it.'

So gathering up his weapons, and grievously bidding his friends farewell, Diarmaid left that hall of sleepers, and found Grainne waiting for him in the night. Together they climbed out of Tara by the spears he fixed in the outer wall, and when they were on the other side, Diarmaid said, 'This is an evil journey you are come on, Grainne, for I know no corner of Ireland that will hide the two of us. It were better for us now that we turn back before Finn wakes.' But Grainne answered him that she herself would never turn back, nor would she ever be parted from him unless it was death itself that parted them.

Then, murmuring with a heavy heart that he would nevertheless keep faith with Finn, Diarmaid led Grainne off into the night. They travelled far, crossing the River Shannon at Athlone, until they came at last to the place called the Wood of the Two Huts. It was there, in the middle of the wood, that Diarmaid made a dwelling for Grainne, with a fence woven out of willow wands and so built that it had seven doors by which they might escape from it.

When Finn woke from his drugged sleep and learned of the flight of Diarmaid and Grainne, he was consumed by a rage so dark that his friends feared for his wits and felt more sympathy for Diarmaid than for their jealous lord. Finn's best trackers were immediately put on the trail of the fugitives and the hiding-place in the wood was quickly discovered. When word was brought back to the Fianna, Oisin and Oscar decided that the lovers must be warned that Finn was coming. They despatched Finn's own hound,

Bran, to lay his head in the lap of Diarmaid where he slept in the bothy, and when he was woken by Bran's touch, Diarmaid knew at once what was meant by the warning. Yet, to Grainne's great dread, he refused to make his escape.

'As I cannot at last avoid Finn,' he said sadly, 'I would as soon he took me now as at any other time,' So the two of them waited together for Finn and his company of paid men to come upon them.

Now Finn knew that those closest to him had no sympathy for his black rage. Even his own son, Oisin, reproached him for his jealousy, but his pride and fury were relentless in their desire for vengeance. From his own deep knowledge it was also clear to him that the fugitives were still inside the bothy in the Wood of the Two Huts; yet when they came there, Oisin tried to dispute it, saying that it was a shameful sign of jealousy in his father's mind to imagine that Diarmaid would stay in a place where he knew Finn was after him.

Looking on his son with a cold eye, Finn strode to the high fence and shouted over it. 'Oisin swears you would not wait in this place with the knowledge that Finn is after you, but I say you are here, Diarmaid. Which of us is in the right of it?'

'When did you ever fail in your good judgement, Finn?' Diarmaid answered at once. 'I am here with Grainne.'

Then Finn ordered his men to surround that place and go in and take them.

Now among the Everliving Ones who watched over the destiny of men it was Aengus Og who took the greatest interest in the affairs of lovers. It was he also who had stood foster father to Diarmaid when the young man had been pupil to Manannan mac Lir in the Land of Promise beneath the wave. Seeing the great peril in which his foster son now stood, Aengus took the cloak of invisibility used by the gods and set out on a cold clear wind till he alighted beside Diarmaid and Grainne where they waited with racing hearts inside the bothy in the wood.

Aengus advised Diarmaid that in this dangerous pass the wise thing was to make use of the magic mantle which he had brought with him. By covering their two heads with it, they could pass invisibly through the lines of Finn's men and thus escape his fury. Yet Diarmaid's loyal heart would not allow him to escape Finn's wrath by these supernatural means.

Asking Aengus to take Grainne under the protection of the cloak that she at least might escape unharmed, he said 'If I live, I will follow you before long, and if I do not, then take Grainne to her father at Tara and let him decide what should best be done with her.'

He watched as the god wrapped the mantle about Grainne, then the two figures vanished before his eyes, and he was left alone with Finn's men waiting for him at all seven gates.

At each of the doors he had built, Diarmaid called out to ask who guarded it, and at five of those gates stood companies led by men sympathetic to his plight – Oisin, Oscar, Caoilte and others, from any of whom he might have asked for aid. The sixth gate was guarded by the clan who had first tracked him down, and they had never had any love for him. Then, when Diarmaid demanded to know who guarded the last gate, and a voice answered, 'No friend to you, Diarmaid, son of Duibhne,' he knew that Finn himself waited for him there, and with four hundred paid men at his back.

'Then it is at your gate I shall come out, Finn,' he shouted, and with the aid of the two javelins that had been given to him long before by Manannan mac Lir, he vaulted high across the wall. The amazing leap left Finn's host stunned with surprise, and when he landed Diarmaid fled so fleetly that they could not catch him. Breathless, he came to the place where Aengus waited with Grainne, who cried out with joy when she saw him safe.

Half a wild boar was roasting over the spit in that little cabin, so Diarmaid ate and rested well that night in Grainne's arms. On the morrow Aengus said that he must leave them, but he gave them this advice: never to hide in a tree with but a single trunk; never to rest in a cave with a single entrance; and never to land on an island with a single harbour. 'And wherever you cook your food,' he said, 'do not eat it in that place; and wherever you eat your food do not lie down to sleep in that place; and wherever you find sleep never lay your heads in that same place again.' Then, consigning them to a life like that of hunted birds, he wished them well and left them.

So faithfully did the fugitives follow the advice of Aengus that it was a long while before Finn's men caught up with them. On their journey westwards they encountered a young warrior looking for a master. His name was Muadan and when he pledged his service to Diarmaid, Grainne urged her lover to accept it, 'for you cannot always be without people,' she said.

So the three of them travelled together and when they came to the coast they saw three ships in a bay with troops of armed men coming ashore. Demanding to know who the foreigners were, Diarmaid learned that two thousand men had been sent for out of Alba by Finn to help him in his search. They were led by three champions called Blackfoot, Whitefoot and Strongfoot, and when they demanded to know if their questioner had seen the two fugitives they sought, Diarmaid said that he had seen them only the day before, and promised the foreigners that they would know Diarmaid's fighting hand when they met it.

Then he asked if there was any wine aboard the ships, and when a great tun was brought ashore, they drank together for a time, and Diarmaid amazed the foreigners with a breathtaking display of athletic feats. When the drunken soldiers tried to stand on the wine tun themselves and emulate his skill at trundling it downhill, fifty of them were killed. On the next day more of them died when he challenged them to leap as he did, nakedly, onto the point of an upright spear. Still more were cut to pieces when they tried to ape the agile way he crossed a bridge made by the edge of that fierce sword, the *Moralltach*, that he had placed between two forked sticks. Then, with the odds against him greatly narrowed, Diarmaid girded on that sword the next day and, leaving Grainne in the protection of his friend Muadan, went out against the foreign army. At the end of the fighting the three champions had few warriors left under their command, though to Grainne's great joy, Diarmaid himself came back uninjured.

When the three champions came against him on the morrow, he defeated each of them in turn. Rather than killing them, he left all three shamefully bound in knots that no one could untie. But there were three savage hounds kept in that company, and knowing that it could not be long before those beasts were loosed after him, Diarmaid told Grainne and Muadan that it would be well if they left the cave where they were dwelling.

Not long afterwards the first of the hounds caught up with them. Muadan stopped it in its tracks by taking from the cover of his cape a small terrier of his own which sprang into the jaws of the great beast, passed down its throat, seized the heart of it in its teeth, and burst out again through the rib-cage at the side. Meanwhile Diarmaid brought down the second hound with a single javelin, but the third leapt over his head with its slavering jaws flashing at Grainne. Before those teeth could reach her, Diarmaid reached up, caught the beast by the hind legs, and brought it down so violently that its brains were dashed out against a rock. With the hounds dead, he turned on the hunters, sparing only one of them, the Woman of the Black Mountain, who brought news of the defeat to Finn.

Meanwhile Finn had been approached by two warriors seeking places among the fighting men of the Fianna. Because they were the sons of men who had brought about his father's death, Finn put a hard ordeal on them. He said he would permit them to join the company of the Fianna only if they accomplished one of two things. Either they must fetch him berries from the magic quicken-tree, whose property was to ward off all sickness and give an ambrosial sense of wellbeing; or they must bring him the head of the traitor Diarmaid. Now it was well known that the quicken-tree was guarded by the one-eyed Fomorian giant, Searbhan, a monster of fearsome power; so of the two tasks, the latter seemed much easier to these warriors. Both would taste defeat, and be tied in knots as Diarmaid's prisoners, before they realized their error.

Now that quicken-tree had grown from a magic rowanberry carelessly dropped by one of the People of Danu in ancient times. It was they who had set Searbhan to guard its fruit and such was the monster's fearsome vigilance that even the men of the Fianna were reluctant to come near the tree. When the two captive warriors recalled that place to Diarmaid's mind, it occurred to him that he and Grainne might at last find safe refuge there. Boldly he confronted the hideous Fomorian sentinel, asking leave to camp and hunt in the land around the quicken-tree. With a surly glance from his single eye, Searbhan replied that they might camp where they pleased so long as they took no berries from the tree he guarded.

By this time Grainne had fallen pregnant and was cruelly suffering from the sickness of it. As she waited for Diarmaid to return from foraging in the country round the tree, she began to crave the comfort that might come from eating its scarlet berries. When he saw how she suffered, Diarmaid went back to Searbhan and asked if, for the sake of her great need, he might not have a handful of the berries as a gift.

The monster answered that if Grainne were the last woman on earth and nothing but those berries would save both her and the unborn child, she still should not have them. Angered by such callous indifference, Diarmaid drew his sword then, and after a long struggle that all but cost him his life, clove the Fomorian monster through the brains. Gathering clutches of the scarlet berries from the tree, he gave some at once to Grainne, and the rest he gave to his prisoners, bidding them return to Finn with them and take their place among the Fianna.

When Finn heard their tale, he gathered his forces once more to seek out his elusive enemy at the magic quicken-tree. By the time he arrived there, Diarmaid and Grainne had left the first shelter they had built and were living like herons among the rowan boughs. Hidden among the leaves, they watched Finn and his men arrive at the glade in the heat of the day and set up camp about the unguarded tree.

Now Finn knew full well where Diarmaid and Grainne were hidden, but when he told Oisin this, his son said it was a shameful mark of great jealousy on his father to imagine that Diarmaid would be hiding in such a place when he knew that Finn was after him. So Finn ordered that his fidchell board be brought out, and when the pieces were put in their places on the board beneath the tree, Finn challenged his son to a game. As play unfolded, Oisin was given advice by Oscar and Finn's druid, but Finn worked his own strategy so skillfully that after a time there was only one move left by which Oisin might win the game. Neither he nor either of his advisors could see it.

From his leafy hiding place in the boughs above the board Diarmaid had watched the progress of the game and – being no mean fidchell player himself – had already seen the winning move. Unable to bear the way Finn taunted Oisin, he plucked a berry from a branch and let it fall on the crucial piece. Oisin's attention was attracted there, he saw the move, made it, and to Finn's chagrin, the men of the Fianna gave a great shout when the game turned so. Two more games ended in the same way. Then, at his third defeat, Finn rose to his feet and shouted, 'Small wonder you win the game, Oisin, when you have help not only from my druid and my grandson, but from the traitor Diarmaid in the tree above you.'

Again Oisin declared that such a jealous fancy was a mark of great shame on his father's mind, but Finn cried out, 'I say you are in the tree with your whore, Diarmaid, and my son, Oisin, says you are not. Which of us is in the right of it?'

Then Diarmaid answered, 'When did your true judgement ever fail you, Finn? I am here in the quicken-tree with Grainne.'

Then he rose up and, in full view of Finn and the Fianna, he gave Grainne three tender kisses on the mouth.

In the intolerable bitterness of his heart, Finn could not bear the sight of it. Fighting against a black swooning in his limbs, he cried out that in return for the great shame that Diarmaid had brought upon him before all the Fianna when he stole Grainne away from the hall at Tara, he would swiftly lose the head that gave those kisses.

With that Finn summoned all his four hundred paid fighting men to surround the tree and promised to give his own arms and armour, together with a place of honour among the Fianna, to the man who brought him the traitor's head.

Again, in this moment of direst need, Aengus Og of the Ever-living Ones, Protector of the Birds, came to the aid of his foster son. Thus it was that, when the first warrior mounted the tree and Diarmaid kicked him out of the boughs with his foot, it was the magic power of Aengus that put the glamour of Diarmaid's own face on the falling man, so that the head was cut off him when he hit the ground. Time and again this happened until the ground about the tree was slippery with heads that no longer bore Diarmaid's fair features. Then once again, at Diarmaid's behest, Aengus wrapped Grainne in the mantle of invisibility and bore her away, while Diarmaid himself vaulted from the tree with a great leap that took him over the heads of Finn's men and gave him start enough to vanish in the forest.

Some say that after Finn's baser nature had suffered this further defeat he went into the otherworld land of Tir Tairngire in search of aid from the hag who had nursed him once when he was a child in arms; and that when he found her there among the shades she promised to return to Ireland and do what was in her power to help him against Diarmaid.

As for the fugitive lovers, they were taken under the protection of Aengus Og for a time, in his dwelling by the river Boyne. After that they concealed themselves in the deep hollow of a sea cave by the western ocean where, on a night of violent storm, a man of the Fomor called Ciach the Fierce sought shelter with them. Diarmaid made him welcome and the two men sat at the gaming-board together; but Ciach had the better of it, and what he asked as his winnings was that Grainne should be his wife.

When he put his arms about her as if to carry her away, Grainne jested that it was a long time since the third man of the Fianna had done as much. Stung with sudden, jealous rage, Diarmaid reached for his sword and struck the Fomor dead. In her own fury at his madness Grainne took a knife that was near her hand and thrust it into Diarmaid's thigh. For a hot moment the two of them stared at one another; then, without uttering a word or a cry, Diarmaid crashed out into the storm.

Crying after him, Grainne followed him out into the night, but if he heard he would not answer her; and it was not until daybreak that she found him. They sat unspeaking in the wild air among the rocks, scarcely together, listening to the sea.

After a time they heard the sharp cry of a heron on the wind. Grainne turned to her silent lover and said quietly, 'Tell me if you can, fair son of Duibhne to whom I gave my love, why is it that the heron cries out?'

Then Diarmaid closed his eyes and said, 'O Grainne, daughter of the High King, you who never took a step aright, it was because she was frozen to the rocks that the bird cried out.'

Then suddenly Grainne was at his side asking forgiveness of him, but he said it was a hard thing she asked, for though she was as beautiful as a tree in flower, her love passed as quickly away. And once having spoken, he reproached her bitterly then for the great fault of bringing this curse of banishment on him. 'I am like a crazed deer, or a beast strayed from the herd, and there is a fierce longing on me to be with my own kind again.' Then all the list of his losses rose in his throat – how for her treacherous sake he had lost his country, his kindred, his honour, his delight in life, and all that was dear to him, and how he had gained nothing in their place but this bitter life of wandering and hunger. 'It would have been better had you given me your hatred,' he said, 'and kept your love for the lord I have lost.'

Then, in the anguish of her love, Grainne was in tears before him, saying that the sight of his face was dearer to her than all the treasures they had lost. 'For the first time I looked on you was as a whole life in a single glance,' she said, 'and all the joy of my heart is there, and I shall know no moment of happiness unless you take me again as it was before; for I know that all the grievous fault of this is mine.'

Yet still she met only the cold shadow of the hardness in his mind. Weeping she begged Diarmaid not to leave, but like a man bewildered he shook his head against her pleas. 'You are a woman full of words,' he said. 'How can I take you again when one day you betray the Head of the Fianna, and on another day you will as lightly betray me?' And nothing Grainne could say would soften the harshness of his speech against her.

So they walked in terrible silence for a time till they came to a place where there was fresh water running among the rocks of a cave, and they were both weary from the grief that was between them. When they had drunk at the spring, Grainne asked Diarmaid if he had no hunger for some bread and meat. He answered roughly that he would eat it if only he had some; but Grainne had what she offered about her, and said to him, 'Give me a knife that I may cut it.'

'Take it from the sheath where you left it,' he said, holding back his cloak, and she saw that the knife was still in his thigh. So Grainne put her hand to the hilt and gently drew the blade out of his flesh. The blood flowed at Diarmaid's thigh; and in all her life Grainne would know no moment of shame more bitter than that.

For a long time after the quarrel they wandered disconsolate throughout Ireland, and each night when Diarmaid rested, Grainne would watch over him, singing those songs that would best help him to sleep; and when he was asleep she would end by singing that the parting of them, if it ever came, would be as the parting of the life from her own body. Then, at first light, when it was time to rouse her sleeping lord, she would sing how the stag was stirring in the ferns and the hornless doe was crying after her fawn; and that the running of Finn's men was so hard upon them that Diarmaid should not let death reach him, nor give himself to sleep for ever.

Then there came a time in a deep cave under Ben Edair when an old woman befriended them. Seeing their plight and their exhaustion, she said she would keep watch over them as they rested; but it was the hag whose help Finn had sought, and she got word to him of the place where she had found Diarmaid and Grainne, and promised to keep them there till he could come upon them with his men.

Before she went back into the cave, the hag drenched her cloak in sea water, and when Diarmaid asked her why it was so wet, she declared that she had never seen a day such as that for cold and storms. Ice had thickened every ford, she said, and every hill-side furrow was a river, and every loch a storm-tossed sea. In the whole world there was shelter in the world for neither deer nor crow, and the three of them were lucky indeed to have this cave with her great pot hanging from its hook above the fire.

Then she left the lovers alone in the deeps of the cave for a time, but her cloak still lay drying where she had left it. When Grainne woke and Diarmaid told her of the strange storm that raved outside, she put her tongue to the cloak and tasted the sea-salt on it.

'Surely the old woman has betrayed us,' she cried. 'Rise up, Diarmaid, and gird your arms about you, for Finn and his men are on their way.'

When they went out of the mouth of the cave the day was bright about them, and they saw Finn and his fighting men advancing across the strand, and no escape because of the great cliff at their backs. Then a cry drew their gaze towards the sea where a boat was putting in at the shore, and a man in a golden yellow cape stood at the helm, who was Aengus come again to help them and take them back with him to Brugh na Boyne.

So the time came when, in the dark passion of his heart, Finn decided to seek out Diarmaid in the dwelling place of Aengus. His old nurse helped him by putting a druid-mist about Finn and the Fianna to bring them there, but strive as they might, the strength of their arms was not enough, and Finn saw that it was only by the power of her enchantments that the life of Diarmaid might be ended there. So one day, while Diarmaid was out hunting alone, the hag concealed herself in the leaf of a water lily that had a hole in it much as a quernstone has; and she made that leaf rise on the wind till it was in the air over Diarmaid, whence she shot down darts at him through the hole. The man was so sorely wounded by the darts that he might soon have died of it; but falling on his back, he took his great spear in his hand and hurled it skywards where it pierced the hole in the leaf and took the life out of the hag beyond it. The body of Finn's nurse fell to the ground, and with his last strength Diarmaid hacked off the wizened head, and brought it back with him to Aengus Og.

It was on the next day that the god Aengus decided that the time had come for peace. He went to where Finn was grieving for the death of his nurse, and made him consider how all his strength of arms, all his knowledge and his guile, together with all the magic powers he could command had brought him no nearer to his vengeance. He told how that desire for vengeance was a terrible thing which had infected Finn's once noble heart; and when he asked Finn if he would not make peace with Diarmaid, the head of the Fianna at last agreed to it. Then Aengus went to Tara where he told Grainne's father, Cormac mac Art, that Finn was ready to make peace with Diarmaid. He asked if the High King of Ireland would not do the same, and when Cormac said that he would, Aengus returned to where Diarmaid and Grainne were, and asked if they too were not ready now for peace. They said they were – 'but only if they meet the conditions I will ask,' said Diarmaid, 'which are that I shall have back the lands my father had, without rights of hunting for Finn on those lands, and without rent or tribute to the King of Ireland; and that Cormac shall freely give to Grainne those lands which are her rightful marriage portion.'

Then it was agreed that, for the sake of peace, those conditions would be granted, and after their sixteen hard years of wandering, Diarmaid and Grainne were allowed to settle far away from Finn and Tara, in a fair place that was called Rath Grainne. Four sons and a daughter were born to them there, and for a long time they lived in such peace that men would say there was no richer man in Ireland, nor one more filled with content than Diarmaid, who had been a wandering outcast once.

As part of the peace settlement a new marriage was arranged between Finn and another of Cormac's daughters, but ever afterwards a residue of bitterness burned in his heart for the shame that Diarmaid had brought on him. Nor was Grainne herself wholly content, for she thought it a shame on the honour of her house that neither the High King her father, nor Finn the first man of the Fianna, ever came there to grace it with their presence.

One day she complained of this to her husband and Diarmaid asked why she would want them to come when she knew the enmity they still bore towards him in their hearts. But how was it ever to be ended, Grainne protested, if no generous or fond-hearted word ever passed between them? 'It is my wish that we give them a great feast here at our home,' she said, 'and that way you will again win their affection.'

So Diarmaid consented to it, and Finn came with all the host of the Fianna to Rath Grainne; and Cormac mac Art, High King of Ireland, came with all his retinue, and a great feasting was made that lasted from night to night throughout the space of a whole year.

On the last night of that festive year Diarmaid heard the voices of hounds at chase sounding through his sleep. When he asked Grainne if she heard the noise, she said that it was only a dream laid on him by the *Tuatha de Danaan*, and he should shake it from him. But on the next morning, Diarmaid rode out to see who it was that hunted on his land. At the crest of Ben Gulbainn he found Finn alone but for his great hound, Bran. Angrily Diarmaid demanded if it was he who had hunted there that night in breach of their agreement. But Finn denied that he had been hunting, saying only that when he had been out exercising his hounds, one of them had lit on the scent of a wild boar. It was a dangerous beast that the Fianna had failed to hunt down many times, and had already killed thirty of his men. Then Finn looked out across the hill and saw where the boar was thundering towards them, driven on by the huntsmen of the Fianna. 'There is danger to you in confronting that boar, Diarmaid,' he said. 'We should leave the hill to him.'

Stung by Finn's condescension, Diarmaid declared that he was not afraid to face a charging boar, and knew no reason why he should not do so.

'Do you not know,' Finn answered him, 'that it was your own father who killed the son of a steward once, and that the steward used his magic power to turn his son's remains into that earless Green Boar, vowing that one day your father's son would die on its tusks?'

'I know nothing of that,' said Diarmaid, 'nor will I quit my own hill because of a boar. Lend me your hound Bran and I will put an end to the beast.'

But Finn would not lend him the hound, saying that Bran had often faced this boar before and could do nothing against it. Then Diarmaid looked Finn long in the eye and said, 'It is in my mind that you made this hunt to find my death, Finn.'

'And if that were so,' Finn answered, 'did you not give me good cause to wish your death when you shamed me before all the Fianna in Tara's hall?'

'And do you still blame me for that, Finn,' said Diarmaid, 'when in all my life I never did anything against you but that one thing? And even that I did only because Grainne put her bonds on me, and I would not fail in my bonds for all the good there might be in the world.' And when Finn did not answer him, he sighed and added, 'Yet if my death is waiting for me here, then there is no use in my fleeing from it.'

So Diarmaid balanced his javelin in his hand, saying, 'It is an unwise thing not to follow the counsel of a good woman, for Grainne bade me bring my great sword, the *Moralltach*, with me this morning, and I did not heed her.' Then he turned away from Finn and advanced across the hill to face the charge of the boar that the huntsmen of the Fianna drove towards him. And when the boar was close upon him he took straight aim and hurled it with all his strength so that the point hit the beast squarely in its tusked face. Yet the spear glanced off that massive head, leaving its bristled hide unscratched, and still it came on at him. So Diarmaid drew the short sword at his side and brought it down over the boar as it reached him; but the blade broke across its back, and the tusks of the boar tore into him as it threw him from his feet, and gored and trampled him so that his bowels were out where he lay on the ground of Ben Gulbain.

With the last of his strength, Diarmaid turned as the force of the boar carried its hot bulk past, and lifting the hilt of the sword that was still in his hand, he hurled it with such despairing fury that it crashed into the back of the boar's skull and smashed its brains. Then Diarmaid lay back in his blood under the heavy sky.

When Finn came up to him, the dying hero said, 'And will you not save me, Finn, for it is well known that water brought in your hands has the power to heal any man not yet dead?'

'I know of no spring on this hill,' Finn answered.

'Not nine steps from where you stand,' Diarmaid gasped, 'is the best spring in all Ireland.'

By this time the huntsmen of the Fianna had come up, with Finn's grandson, Oscar, at their head; and when Oscar heard this and saw that Finn still did not move he urged him to bring the water to his dying friend without delay. So Finn went to the spring and gathered water in his cupped hands, but as he stared into the little pool his thoughts darkened and by the time he came back to where Diarmaid lay, all the water had slipped away between his fingers.

With the blood already at his mouth, Diarmaid said, 'Is your heart still so hard against me, Finn? Will you not bring me some water now?'

So Finn returned to the spring and filled his hands again, but again the thought of Grainne darkened his mind, and his hands were empty on his return. A piteous sigh broke from Diarmaid's throat then, and Oscar stood before Finn saying, 'I beg you to bring him some water, Finn, for if you do not, I vow that one or other of us will die beside him on this hill.'

Finn hastened back to the spring then; and when he returned the cup of his healing hands was filled, but even as he knelt beside the man who had been both his enemy and his friend, the breath passed out of Diarmaid, and all the men of the Fianna gave out three shouts for the grievous pity of that death.

Then Oscar stared at Finn, saying that the loss of Diarmaid was felt greater now than if even Finn himself had died. 'Never would I have joined this hunt on Ben Gulbain,' he said, 'if I had known it was against Diarmaid that you made it.'

But Finn answered only that they should leave that hill before the *Tuatha de Danann* came upon them there. 'For though we had no hand in Diarmaid's death,' he said, 'Aengus will not believe the truth of it from our lips.'

So the men of the Fianna gathered up Diarmaid's broken body and brought it back to where Grainne was. A great cry broke out of her, and then the keening of all the women of the Fianna rang about those hills. That night Grainne made a song of her grief over the dead body of Diarmaid, cursing the day when she gave him her love and came between Finn and his noble soul, and brought about the sorrowful story of this death.

She would have had Diarmaid laid to rest at their home in Rath Grainne, but the grieving god, Aengus, came to claim the hero's body, ruing the single night in all those long years that he had failed to give Diarmaid his protection.

So Diarmaid was taken at last to Brugh na Boyne, home of the gods, where even in death he might be friend and companion to Aengus still.

Some time after the first deep grief of all of this had passed, Finn came secretly to Grainne and spoke softly to her. At first, in the rage and hatred of her heart, she would hear no word he said, and every hard word that leapt to her own tongue she uttered at him, holding back nothing of the hate and fury that she felt. But Finn endured all, and outlasting the rage of her heart, spoke ever more softly to her, till in the end he brought her to his will.

Some say that he could do this only because he had put a great enchantment of love on Grainne; others that it happened only because the mind of a woman changes like a running stream. Yet whatever the truth of it may be, it is known that Grainne eventually persuaded the sons of Diarmaid to make their peace with Finn; and Finn and Grainne stayed together to the end.

5

The Shoes of the Leprechaun

In the days when Fergus mac Leide ruled over Ulster from his court at Emain Macha, there dwelt in the deeps of Loch Rudraige a huge water-monster that was a cause of dread and terror to all the land around. From the turbulent way the scaled coils of its body stirred the waters of the mere as though a violent tempest blew across the lake, the monster came to be called the Sineach, which in English means the 'Stormy One'.

The lives of many boatmen were horribly lost when the jaws of the creature dragged them down into its lair beneath the waves, and the people of Ulster had great grief because of it. Then a day came when the boat of the king himself was attacked as he crossed the loch. Wreathed in slime, the vile devouring head broke the surface, capsizing the boat. Though Fergus fought bravely against it, there was no ground under his feet to lend strength to his sword-arm; so lashing out with its talons and evilly spiked tail, the Sineach closed its teeth on the helmsman, and sank back beneath the waves unscathed. Fergus himself escaped with his life that day, but his face was left so cruelly mutilated by the struggle that the skin of his mouth was twisted round to the back of his head.

Once a handsome man, he was now hideous to look upon. Yet none dared reflect in their own features the revulsion they felt on seeing his face; and fearful of the harm that might come to the king's mind if he ever saw the full horror of what had been done to him, his counsellors had all the mirrors in Emain Macha secretly removed. So for a long time Fergus went in ignorance of the fearful spectacle he presented wherever he showed his face. But truth will not stay hidden long, and some say it was the king's barber that let him know of his deformity, and some say that the king's wife scorned him for it in their bed one night; but whoever it was, and however it happened, Fergus learned the terrible truth of what had been done to his face, and thereafter a still fiercer loathing for the monstrous creature in Loch Rudraige shrivelled his heart.

From that time onwards he had thought for nothing except how to come at the Sineach with the full force of his great sword, the Caladcolg, and thereby take his vengeance on it. Yet the more he pondered the problem, the less soluble it seemed, and the bitter frustration of it darkened all his hours.

Now while Fergus was king among the Ulstermen in Emain Macha, the realm of the leprechauns was ruled by a high and mighty fellow called Iubdan, who was often heard to boast that nowhere in all the green isle of Erin was there a king who ruled over a finer, wealthier and more powerful court than he.

There was a bard in that court called Eisirt who had long known that his own learning made him much wiser in the ways of the wide world than his braggart king, and the sound of such bragging was as a knife on slate to Eisirt's ears. Nevertheless he thought it politic to possess his soul in patience, but a day came when he could stand Iubdan's bluster no more.

'Sure if the king ever travelled beyond his own court as far as the land of Ulster,' he said, 'he would learn that his own royal palace is as a tiny hovel before Emain Macha, and that King Fergus mac Leide is mightier far than he, as is the oak over the gillyflower. For is it not well known that even the feeblest peasant in Ulster is as a giant in size beside the stature of the tallest leprechaun?'

For a time after he had spoken a great gasp of silence held the whole of Iubdan's hall in the gape of its mouth. No one had dared to speak to the king this way before. Now it was for the king himself to find the breath to speak, and when he did so it was with a face blackened by rage and a hot light of fury in his eyes. Had he not always known Eisirt for a liar and a traitor, he said, and why should any loyal leprechaun pay such seditious gossip heed unless the bard himself went out into Ulster and brought back living proof of what he said?

Now it is an unwise thing to offend a poet, and with a cold flame of resentment in his heart, Eisirt set out to bring back such evidence as would expose the king for the fool and braggart that he was.

Out of the realm of the leprechauns he went, and came at last to Fergus' court at Emain Macha, where his diminutive appearance was a cause for astonishment to who all looked upon the little fellow there. Though everything around him was of titan size, Eisirt himself was least surprised of all, because he knew why he was there and had known what to expect when he came out of his own land into that gigantic world.

Now this was in the days before Fergus had taken his injury from the Sineach, and the king was still at peace with himself; so he received this unexpected embassy from the leprechauns with an open mind and heart. When Eisirt explained his mission and asked for an ambassador to return to Iubdan with him, it was decided that only the king's dwarf, Aedh, could possibly fulfil that mission. Yet the plain fact was that even he, who was scarcely half a grown man's height, could have sat the little bard on his shoulder and hardly felt the weight of him. But the dwarf was also an affable fellow and when the king asked him if he would travel into the land of the leprechauns, Aedh readily agreed to go for the adventure of the thing.

For three days and nights Eisirt was liberally treated as an extraordinary guest at Emain Macha, and passed the time inquisitively exploring there. Then accompanied by the dwarf Aedh, the bard of the leprechauns set off triumphantly across Ireland, back to the tiny realm where Iubdan ruled.

When they reached the shores of the sea, Aedh caught a glimpse of a small creature approaching them over the waves, but even his keen eyes could not make out what it might be.

'Is that a hare coming towards us across the sea?' he asked.

'Indeed it is not,' Eisirt replied, 'it is the horse of King Iubdan which will carry us home.'

It is not hard to imagine the shock and terror of the court when the bard Eisirt returned to Iubdan's palace bringing with him this immense specimen of the scale of things in the court of Fergus mac Leide at Emain Macha.

Struggling to conceal his fear and chagrin, Iubdan looked up to where Aedh loomed high over him with a smile wider than a gate, and found himself admitting in his secret thought that Ulster must truly be a land of giants.

'Yet in the powerful country whence he comes,' Eisirt triumphantly proclaimed, 'my friend Aedh here has only the stature of a dwarf. His royal master, King Fergus – also my good friend –

stands more than twice that size.' He paused a moment for effect, and then, remembering the public slight he had taken at Iubdan's mouth, he turned away from the king to where all the assembled court cowered in Aedh's great shadow. 'I concede, however,' he added cunningly, 'that I have brought no proof of that; but I felt sure that our own mighty king would prefer to take his queen with him into Ulster and be royally received by Fergus himself.'

Iubdan knew that both his reputation and his throne were now at risk. Glancing at his wife, Queen Bebo, for reassurance, he found none there; nevertheless he gulped out a declaration that, in their own good time, he and his queen would certainly grace the court of Fergus with their regal presence.

'Excellent!' Eisirt exclaimed, 'Then you will certainly taste the porridge from the great iron cauldron hanging in the kitchen there, and when you return we can discuss its merits together.'

Aedh was sent back to Emain Macha with the news that Fergus should prepare his court for a state visit by leprechaun royalty, and the bard Eisirt lost no public opportunity to air his knowledge of the marvels that awaited Iubdan there. The discomfited king listened in silence, regretting only that the pressure of state business prevented him from leaving quite as soon as he would like. But all the joy had gone out of Iubdan's life. No longer could he strut his kingdom, congratulating himself on all its glories; and the time came when the journey could no longer be postponed. So, in a calamitous state of concealed apprehension, Iubdan and Bebo made their way out of their own small kingdom into the vast realms of Fergus.

They made sure that they approached Emain Macha under cover of darkness, and when they saw in the gloom the massive size of everything around them, their hearts quailed with greater terror than before. Queen Bebo was all for leaving that monstrous place at once, but Iubdan insisted they must explore as much as they dare for Eisirt would be sure to test their knowledge of Emain

Macha on their return. Furtive as house mice they crept from room to vast room, till they came at last to the king's kitchen where the huge iron cauldron hung on its hook. It was filled with what seemed to them a thick lake of porridge ready for Fergus to break his fast on the morrow.

'Eisirt has tasted this porridge,' Iubdan said. 'If I cannot discuss its flavours with him he will know I have not kept my word.' So he clambered up the tall stand holding the fire-bars from which the cauldron hung, then gingerly he lowered his feet towards the rim. Balanced there, he was bending to make good his grip when his foot slipped on the greasy edge and, unable to help himself, he tumbled down into the pot.

Choked, blinded and spluttering for a time, his head finally found air again. But strive as he might, there was no way he could lift himself back round the curve of the pot. Nor was Bebo strong enough to climb to the rim herself and balance there while she tried to haul him out. So there was nothing for it but that Iubdan should spend the rest of the night treading porridge, and struggling to keep his regal head above the surface, until daybreak when the first of Fergus' scullions came into the kitchen. To his utter astonishment the lad found the two terrified and exhausted leprechauns there before him.

So Iubdan and Bebo graced the court of Fergus with their presence after all. But that bitter king was in no mood to accord them the same warm welcome he had shown to Eisirt, for since that last visit by a leprechaun, Fergus had suffered the terrible attack by the Sineach, and even more recently he had learned of the true condition of his face.

When he looked down at Iubdan and his wife from his own hideously damaged features, he saw only two shivering creatures that might claim to be a king and queen but had come like thieves in the night to pilfer porridge from his cauldron. Such was the behaviour not of royalty but of churls, and Fergus was of a mind to put the terrified leprechauns to churl's work about the place, had not Queen Bebo burst into a small torrent of tears. Her soft hands were unused to such work she wailed, and the indignity of it would burst her lord's proud heart.

Hearing this, the men and women of Emain Macha laughed out loud for the first time in a long while, and said that in those dark times it would be a pity not to have the amusement of their presence in the court. So Fergus was constrained to take pity on them. If Iubdan gave his royal word that they would not seek to escape, he said, then he and his wife might live the honourable life of hostages in Emain Macha. Having small choice in the matter, Iubdan agreed, and the two leprechauns resigned themselves to life in that titanic land.

Eventually the failure of the king and queen to return became a growing cause for concern and agitation in the realm of the leprechauns. Iubdan may have had his faults, they agreed, but he had preserved a fine sense of the dignity of the kingdom and it was a valorous heart that had led him to venture into the giant land of Ulster with his wife. Even Eisirt, who had fallen under suspicion of foul treachery, was forced to agree that ways must be found to persuade Fergus to release his hostages.

It was on his advice that an embassy to Fergus made a fair-spoken offer. In return for the immediate liberty of their king and queen, the leprechauns undertook to enchant all the fallow plain round Emain Macha so that it would produce a bounteous crop of corn, and without the least need for sowing.

But the Fergus that Eisirt encountered this time was not the man he had met before, for the king's mind had grown as gloomy and stubborn as his outward features were hideous.

If he were to make such a bargain, Fergus scowled, his subjects would grow lazy, and idleness was ever the seedbed of trouble. Besides, one of the few pleasures left to him in life was the sport of watching Iubdan and Bebo primping themselves about Emain Macha. He would not release them.

But not all power lies with the giants of this world. When Fergus refused the fair offer of the leprechauns, their own thoughts turned darker. They decided that if Fergus would not respond to friendly overtures, then affliction might move him.

Not long after Eisirt had been sent back to the leprechauns with a cold answer, the herdsmen of Ulster found the supply of milk from their cattle mysteriously running dry. After a time it became clear that the little people were coming by night and urging the calves to visit their mothers and suck what was rightfully theirs. Nor did the leprechauns deny that they were responsible for this mischief. If Fergus freed their king and queen, they declared, the milk would flow again.

But in his stubborn rage, Fergus was not about to be browbeaten by leprechauns, and again the bargain was refused. Then the springs of Ulster were so fouled that their water was scarcely drinkable. Iubdan and Bebo remained captive still. Inexplicable fires broke out on mill beams and in kilns. The hostages were not released. Overnight all the ears of corn were cut from the stems in the harvest fields, and though the farmers were in despair over the loss, their complaints could not move Fergus' embittered heart.

Driven to extremes, the next delegation of leprechauns threatened that if Iubdan and Bebo were not released at once, all the men and women of Ulster would wake one morning to find themselves shorn bald.

Fergus said that if that were to happen his hostages would certainly be killed.

Hearing this, and understanding by now that threats and menaces would never move the morose king, Iubdan persuaded the legation to go home. Then, having learned from his time in Emain Macha what lay at the root of Fergus' stubborn temper, the leprechaun asked leave to speak with him. He told Fergus that among his possessions in his own kingdom were many rare and precious things. If he and his wife were allowed to go home, then Fergus might take his pick from them.

Fergus asked what possible treasure a leprechaun might have that would be of interest to him. So, one by one, Iubdan listed the treasures he had prized so highly when he was at liberty in his own realm; yet at the loving description of each one of them, Fergus merely shook his head. But Iubdan had cleverly kept till last the item he thought likeliest to tempt the king.

'Then perhaps your majesty might wish to have my finest pair of shoes,' he said.

Fergus laughed gruffly at that. 'And why should I have the smallest desire for a leprechaun's shoes?'

'Perhaps because those shoes are enchanted with a special property.'

'And what property might that be?'

'With those shoes,' Iubdan answered quietly, 'even a man of your own great size might easily walk on water.' Then he looked at Fergus with a knowing glance.

At once Fergus saw how such shoes might solve at last the problem of how to come at the Sineach, and take his vengeance for the foul injury it had wrought on him. 'Could I walk with them across Loch Rudraige?' he demanded.

'You could walk with them to Alba,' Iubdan answered.

'And could I stand firmly in them on the waves?'

'As any rock,' said Iubdan.

'Then have those shoes brought to me,' said Fergus, 'and liberty is yours.'

As soon as he had the precious shoes in his possession, Fergus girded on his famous sword, the Caladcolg, and went down to the shores of Loch Rudraige.

There he stepped out lightly onto the quiet water and found that what Iubdan had promised him was true. A few yards out, with a fathom of water under him, he stood and flourished his sword. His stance stayed firm as any rock. So with mounting confidence he strode out across the lake till he came to the place where he could feel the turbulence of the Sineach in the deeps beneath him. Then, standing with his feet firmly planted on the waves, he waited for the monster to raise its evil head.

The fight that followed was as terrible to hear as to behold. Uttering its great watery bellow from its massive lizard head, the Sineach writhed all its coils to come at Fergus; but the king had nimbleness on his side as he strode across the water, striking the great beast again and again with the edge of his sword. Yet he could not avoid its talons and teeth entirely, and many and vicious were the gashes he took about his body, before the injured beast finally began to tire of the conflict and sought to withdraw across the loch to lick its wounds.

Scenting victory, Fergus gathered his strength and hastened after it. Each blow he struck drove the Sineach ever closer to the shallows, till the monster ran aground, writhing in agony against the gravel. For a while longer it lashed out with desperate, exhausted rage against its unrelenting assailant, then a sweeping blow from the great sword Caladcolg all but severed its neck. Black blood gushed from the wound, and the huge, wrecked beast lay gasping and dying on the shore. Avoiding as best he could, the last tearing flail of its claws, Fergus came up beside the body of the Sinneach, thrust his blade deep inside the flesh, and cut out its heart.

So Loch Rudraige was finally cleansed of the monster that had infested it so long, and Fergus had his vengeance for the dreadful damage wreaked upon his face. But even as he staggered ashore from his victory, the exhausted king was losing so much blood that he could scarcely stand. When he swooned on the strand and lay there with blood leaking unstaunchably from his wounds, it was evident that his death was come upon him.

With the little breath remaining to him, Fergus asked that his sword, the Caladcolg, be set aside, and not brought out again till some hero worthy of it should come to wield its blade in Ulster's cause. Then the life passed out of him.

His grieving people buried him beneath the soil of his land, and a great stone was set up over his grave on which an inscription carved in Ogham letters recorded for all time the glory of his famous name.

PART TWO

WELSH MYTHS

6

The Head of Annwn

The oldest stories of the British gods tell of the family of Pwyll who was a Prince of Dyfed, that wild region of south-western Wales which was long known to the bards as the Land of Illusion and the Realm of Glamour, and whose rugged, shining coastline borders the dark otherworld kingdom of Annwn.

Pwyll kept court at Arberth, and it was there late one day that the desire came over his heart to go hunting in the wild valley of Glyn Cuch. So he set out with his companions, camped with them that night in Pen Llwyn Diarwya, and rode out again at first light to loose his pack in the valley. As he followed the belling hounds at speed through thick woodland, Pwyll found himself separated from his companions. Winding his horn to gather the hunt and listening for a reply, he heard the sound of another pack baying through the trees towards him.

Moments later a stag of twelve tines crashed through the misty brakes into the clearing where his own hounds had checked. The great beast skidded to a halt, wide-eyed, trembling, the breath

steaming at its muzzle. Pwyll scarcely had time to take in the magnificent sight before the strange pack burst out of the trees after
the stag and dragged it to the ground. Never had Pwyll seen
hounds like these before. For a time he stood spellbound by the
gleam of their white pelts and the glistening redness of their ears
as they clamoured over the fallen stag. But when no huntsman
appeared after them, Pwyll beat off the strange hounds and baited
his own pack on their quarry.

Looking up from the kill he saw a man ride into the glade on a
large dappled grey horse. A hunting-horn was slung about his neck
and he wore a dark grey garment fashioned for the hunt. Reining in
his horse, the grey rider accused Pwyll of unsportsmanlike discour-
tesy in calling off the hounds that had cornered the stag, then bait-
ing his own pack on another man's rightful prey.

'I will take no vengeance for this,' he declared, 'but I will dishonour you to the worth of a hundred stags.'

Mortified, Pwyll replied at once that he would do everything in
his power to redeem his fault and win the man's friendship.

'How will you redeem it?' the stranger asked.

'According to your rank and dignity,' Pwyll answered, 'though I
don't know what that is, nor your name, nor where you come from.'

'I am Arawn,' the stranger told him, 'King of Annwn.'

'Then how might the King of Dyfed win your friendship?'

'There is yet another king in Annwn, whose name is Hafgan,'
said Arawn. 'His lands lie against mine and he wars against me
continually. You can win my friendship only by going to Annwn
and ridding me of his oppression.'

Pwyll said he would gladly do that if only Arawn would show
him how he might come into Annwn.

'That is easily done,' the hunter-king answered. 'I shall put the
shape of my own appearance on you. Thus you shall enter Annwn,
and the fairest woman you ever looked upon will think you myself

and take you to her bed; nor will any man know you from myself. And you will be kept under that enchantment for a year and a day, when you and I will meet in this same place again.'

'But how shall I know Hafgan?' Pwyll asked.

'It is arranged that a year from tonight he and I will meet at the ford. Go there in my place and fight in my cause. But give him only a single blow, and no matter how much he begs you to finish him off with another, do not strike him again, for his strength will only return with that second blow.'

So Pwyll committed himself to this adventure, asking only what would become of his own kingdom during the year he was absent from it. Arawn answered that he would rule Dyfed in Pwyll's place and that no one there would know that it was not Pwyll himself who reigned over them. Then he brought Pwyll to the place where he might enter Annwn and put an enchantment on him that gave him Arawn's own grey-garbed appearance before swiftly returning to Dyfed in the likeness of Pwyll himself.

When Pwyll entered Arawn's magnificent hall in the dark realm of Annwn the servants hastened to meet him showing no surprise at his appearance, and bringing him fresh clothing. So he washed and went into dinner where he was greeted with warm, wifely affection by the loveliest and most spirited woman he had ever seen. A meal served on dishes of gold passed happily enough in gracious, witty conversation between them until the time came for them to go to bed.

Knowing how powerfully he desired the woman, Pwyll could see no other way of keeping faith with his friend Arawn than by turning his back on her at once and lying in fraught stillness till sheer weariness dragged him at last into sleep. So not a word was exchanged between them the entire night, though on the next day affectionate tender relations were speedily resumed. The same thing happened on the next night, and on every following night of a year in which Pwyll spent his days ruling Arawn's kingdom justly, then hunting through the shadowy woods and feasting to his heart's content. Eventually the year was over and the time was come to encounter Hafgan at the ford.

Still bearing the appearance of Arawn, Pwyll was brought there by his companions from the court and found Hafgan waiting for him in the gloom. A strange horseman announced that the duel would be one of single combat with the lands of both contenders at issue. No one else was to interfere.

Silently the two men waded towards each other across the dark ford. Pwyll shattered his opponent's shield with his first blow, and the sword sliced on through into Hafgan's chest giving him so deep a wound that he must surely die of it. Falling into the water at Pwyll's thighs, Hafgan lifted his shocked, agonized gaze demanding that Arawn spare him further suffering by giving him his death-blow.

'I may already live to regret the blow I gave you,' Pwyll said. 'You will take no other at my hand.'

With the life ebbing out of him, Hafgan told his followers that he could no longer maintain his rule over them, and bade them give their allegiance to Arawn. So Afgan's men knelt before Pwyll, saying that the realm of Annwn would henceforth have no other ruler but he.

By noon of the following day Pwyll had secured both parts of Annwn in Arawn's name. With his task completed, he tenderly kissed Arawn's wife for the last time before riding out to keep the appointed meeting in the glade at Glyn Cuch.

Arawn was waiting for him there. Already aware of Pwyll's success, the true King of Annwn thanked Pwyll for his friendship and told him that he would find what had been done for him when he came back to Dyfed. Then the two men resumed their own shapes and each returned to his own kingdom.

When Pwyll rode back to Arberth his friends greeted him as though he had been absent for no more than the length of that day, and when he came to look over his kingdom he found that its seven cantrefs[1] had never been so prosperous as during the past year. Only then did he tell his friends of his adventure and of the debt of gratitude they owed to the King of Annwn.

Meanwhile, on returning to his own shadowy land, Arawn found the whole of Annwn happily united under his rule. He feasted well with his nobles that night, and went off gladly to bed with his wife who was astonished to see him turn warmly towards her and take her into his embrace. She lay in silence, puzzling over this sudden inexplicable change in his behaviour, and for all her husband's loving approaches he could win no response from her. At last he asked her why she would not speak to him.

'What do you expect of me,' she answered, 'when you treat me courteously enough each day, yet for a whole year now you have neither touched nor spoken gently to me in this bed?'

Then Arawn realized what a true and steadfast friend he had found in Pwyll, Prince of Dyfed. Turning to his wife he told her the whole story of what had happened during the past year and how she had shared her bed with a stranger who, though he had worn his own form, had taken no advantage of the deception.

1 A cantref was a division of the kingdom.

Then his wife agreed that Pwyll was a worthy friend indeed, and after that the bonds of friendship between the two men grew even stronger. Gifts were sent between them from one country to the other – hawks and hounds and horses, and whatever each thought the other's heart might desire. And because of the valour and justice of Pwyll's deed in uniting the divided otherworld of Annwn, he was no longer known as Prince of Dyfed, but as Pwyll Pen Annwn – the Wise One who is Head of the Otherworld.

Now outside Pwyll's great hall at Arberth there was an ancient mound of strange, magical character. If a man were to sit on it one of two things would happen to him: either he would be battered by blows from some invisible force or he would be shown a wonder. With things going so well in his domain Pwyll decided the time had come to risk the experience of the mound. He was not afraid of a few blows if they came and he had an appetite for wonders. So watched by a few companions he climbed on to the mound.

As he sat down in that enchanted place no threat of violence stirred the air about his head, but peering into the sudden mist about him he saw a figure appear in the near distance. A woman wearing a shining mantle of gold brocade rode a pale white horse at a steady, ambling pace along the road leading past the mound. Staring at her in fascination, Pwyll asked his companions if any of them knew who she was. None did, so he bade one of them go down to the road and greet her in his name.

The man walked down to intercept the rider at the road but by the time he reached it she had already ambled past. So he jogged after the horse and still came no closer. The faster he ran, the greater seemed to stretch the distance between himself and his goal even though the white mare's steady pace had not sharpened at all. At last, panting and exhausted, he watched the rider vanish from sight and had no choice but to return to the mound with his report of failure.

Intrigued by his account, Pwyll decided to try the enchantment of the mound again the following day. Again the rider appeared, but this time Pwyll had a horseman waiting for her. He was mounted on the swiftest steed in Pwyll's stable, while the woman rode the same large-hooved mare at the same ambling pace. So he trotted gently to accost her and, when he found she had already passed him, cantered to overtake her. Soon he was urging his mount to gallop in pursuit of the strange rider. He pushed his horse so hard that it flagged from the heat of the chase, yet he had still not halved the distance between himself and the ambling mare. So he tried following at a slower pace and made no better progress. After wearing out his mount with a last vain sprint to catch the rider before she disappeared, he too returned in astounded defeat.

That night Pwyll could not put the mystery out of his mind. Sure that the rider must have some purpose in coming there, he returned to the mound again on the next day, determined to pursue her himself this time. Yet he too could overtake her neither by straining after speed nor by matching her own unhurried pace. Baffled, aware that his horse was suffering beneath him, he cried out across the distance between them. 'Maiden, for the sake of him you love best, I beg you to stop.'

Immediately the rider reined in her mount and turned to him saying she would gladly do so and that it would have been better for his horse if he had asked her sooner. When Pwyll asked who she was and why she had come there, she pulled back her riding-veil and he was gazing on a demure, uncertain face that quickened his heart more than any he had ever seen.

'I have come about my own affairs in search of none but your-self,' she said, 'and am truly glad to find you.' Then she told him her name was Rhiannon, and that her father, Hefydd the Ancient, wanted to marry her against her will to a wealthy lord called Gwawl. 'Yet I have told my father I care for none but the Head of Annwn, and I will give myself to Gwawl only if you reject me.' Gazing up at him again, she said, 'I have come to hear your answer, whether you will have me or not.'

'Then hear it,' Pwyll said, 'for if I had the pick of all the fair women in the world I would choose only you.'

'If that is truly so,' Rhiannon answered, 'will you promise to meet me in marriage at a time I appoint?'

Pwyll replied that the sooner that time came the happier he would be; but Rhiannon bade him be patient till a year had passed from that very day. Then he must come to Hefydd's hall where she would have prepared a feast for him. So vowing to keep that appointment, Pwyll let her go. When he returned to his friends he would tell them nothing about his encounter with the maiden no matter how eagerly they questioned him.

The year passed and Pwyll rode in great state as one of a hundred riders to the hall of Hefydd the Ancient, where exuberant preparations had been made to welcome him. Scarcely able to believe his own good fortune in securing Pwyll as his son-in-law, Hefydd had stinted on nothing to provide entertainment for his guests. When they came to the tables that night, Hefydd sat on one side of the Head of Annwn, while his daughter Rhiannon, all the lovelier for this happy fulfillment of her hopes, kept Pwyll still closer company on the other.

The feasting was well begun when the door opened and a tall auburn haired young man came in wearing a bright garment richly brocaded in gold that outshone everyone there. In high good humour, Pwyll demanded that room be made at the table for the resplendent newcomer, but the young man declined the offer, saying he had come only to ask a boon of the Head of Annwn.

'On this happy night you shall have whatever is in my power to give,' said Pwyll, extravagantly opening his hands and turning to Rhiannon for approval. He met only the anguish in her face. 'Why did you give him such an answer?' she said.

'He has given it,' said the newcomer, 'in the clear hearing of all.'

Troubled by Rhiannon's dismay, Pwyll turned back to the stranger. 'Friend,' he demanded, 'tell me what you desire.'

'She whom you would sleep with tonight,' the young man answered. 'My name is Gwawl son of Clud, and Rhiannon was promised first to me. The boon you have granted is her hand in marriage and this whole wedding-feast to be mine.'

Struck dumb with horror, Pwyll turned helplessly to the woman he loved. Stricken and distraught herself, with her lovely head held between her hands, Rhiannon looked away from him saying, 'Did ever man use his wits less well than this?'

Thinking now that it might have been better for the Head of Annwn to take the blows on the mound at Arberth rather than win such happiness and throw it so carelessly away, Pwyll could only protest that he had not known who the supplicant was.

'Nevertheless your word is given,' Rhiannon answered. 'If shame is not to fall on your great name, you must give me to him now.'

'I shall never do that,' Pwyll exclaimed.

'Then your word will be worthless. Give me to him,' Rhiannon whispered fiercely, 'and trust that he shall never have me.'

Uncertain of her meaning, the bewildered Head of Annwn sat at that speechless table with a tongue like stone.

'It is time I had my answer,' said Gwawl, 'or men will know how little honour there is in the Head of Annwn.'

'I do not take back my given word,' said Pwyll at last. 'Rhiannon is yours.'

'Together with all this great feast to celebrate our wedding?' Gwawl insisted triumphantly.

But it was Rhiannon who answered. 'That is not in Pwyll's power to give. All these guests are here at my bidding, the feast is mine, and I did not prepare it for you. Though it has cost him dearly, the Head of Annwn has kept all his given word, Gwawl son of Clud. But it is my word that you shall not take me in marriage till another year has passed. Come again to claim me then.'

So without the bride he had hoped for but with his promises secure, Gwawl went away from Hefydd's hall that night back into his own abundant lands.

Meanwhile in great grief at the rash way in which he had forfeited all happiness, the Head of Annwn came to make his own farewell to Rhiannon.

'Rather would I have shared your bed tonight than watch you leave like this,' Rhiannon said as Pwyll stood stricken before her. 'Yet I bid you return in a year's time also,' she added, 'and when you come hide your companions outside the hall, and wear only a beggar's clothing, and bring with you this bag to be filled with food from Gwawl's feasting table. Then you will see what shall come to pass.'

So resigning himself to trust in the power of the woman that he loved, Pwyll returned to Arberth and waited out the long year till it was time to return to Hefydd's hall.

In great triumph of heart, Gwawl son of Clud came to the hall that day and found Rhiannon and her father waiting for him. Another great banquet had been prepared and this time it was Gwawl who sat in the seat of honour as the feast unfolded.

When the meat was on the table and the wine flowing among the guests, a beggar in shabby garments wearing rag-boots at his feet presented himself at the table craving a boon of Gwawl.

Smiling at Rhiannon, Gwawl turned to the beggar and said, 'I will grant whatever you ask, friend, so long as the request is within reason.'

'I ask only the fill of this small bag with food from your great feast to keep want at bay,' said the beggar.

'A reasonable enough request,' Gwawl replied and ordering the attendants to fill the bag, he turned back to Rhiannon. After a time he noticed to his surprise that the bewildered attendants were still pouring food into the open neck of the bag. The longer he watched, the more they put in, yet the capacity of the bag seemed in no way diminished. 'Will your bag never be filled, friend?' he demanded in some irritation.

Then Rhiannon got to her feet. 'I think you are deceived, Gwawl,' she said. 'I know that bag. It has the property that it will never be filled till a wealthy man treads down its load with his own feet.' She held his eyes then. 'There is none here wealthier than yourself. If you would save our feast you must tread down the food.'

Seeing how rapidly the table was depleted of its fare, and discerning a hint of challenge in Rhiannon's voice, Gwawl got up from his place, told the beggar to hold the neck of the bag open and climbed inside. Instantly Pwyll slipped the bag up over Gwawl's head and knotted its mouth. Thus it was that Gwawl, whose name means 'Light', found himself trapped in the darkness by the Head of Annwn, while Pwyll threw off his grubby robe, unslung his horn, and summoned his men into the hall.

'What do you have there in the bag?' they asked.

'A badger,' Pwyll answered, 'much in need of beating.'

So one by one the lords of Dyfed came up to the writhing bag to kick it or beat it with sticks till Gwawl's groans rang loud about the hall. Thus the brutal game of 'Badger in the Bag' was played for the first time, and with more justice then than ever after. Yet as Gwawl's cries grew more piteous in his pleading that this was no proper death for a noble lord, Hevydd the Ancient interceded on his behalf, saying it would be great shame if a guest were to die in his house that way. So Pwyll turned to Rhiannon and said he would leave the decision on Gwawl's fate to her greater wisdom.

'Then let him stay in the bag,' said Rhiannon, 'unless he yields up all claim to me and acknowledges this marriage-feast as rightly yours.'

'He shall have all,' Gwawl howled from the bag, 'I renounce all claims.'

'And let him further forgo all rights of vengeance for what he has suffered here tonight, and give rich sureties for that into my father's hand.'

'Draw up your terms,' groaned Gwawl. 'I will accept them.'

Then Pwyll opened the bag and Gwawl crawled out among the straw all bruised and bloody, asking leave only to dress his wounds and leave that hall for his own land.

Then as the Head of Annwn once again took the place of honour between his wife and her father, the wedding-feast was resumed with great merriment and joy; and when the revelry was at its height, Pwyll and Rhiannon withdrew to their bed where they passed the night in rapturous contentment.

After another whole day of feasting and merriment, Pwyll sought leave of Hevydd the Ancient to return to Dyfed with his wife. For the next two years they ruled the seven cantrefs together in tranquil prosperity; but when, in the third year, there was still no sign of the queen providing the kingdom with an heir, the nobles of the land began to murmur that Rhiannon was under the curse of Gwawl's kinsmen. Eventually they found the courage to confront the Head of Annwn himself with their complaint. Greatly as they loved him, they said, Pwyll would not be with them for ever, and the land must have an heir to ensure peaceful continuity of rule. If Rhiannon could not give him a son, then let him take a wife who could.

Aggrieved by their complaint, and knowing how Rhiannon had suffered from two late miscarriages, Pwyll reminded them of his great love for his wife and how Dyfed had profited by her wisdom. The royal marriage was not far advanced in years, he said, and he and Rhiannon might still have the joy of a child together. Let the nobles cease their murmuring, and if there was no heir within a year, then he would speak with them again.

To Pwyll's great joy and relief, Rhiannon bore him a son before that year was out. So precious was the child to both land and parents that on the night following the birth no less than six women were set to watch over the exhausted mother and her infant son. Yet every one of them had fallen asleep before midnight and when they woke at cockcrow it was to find the child had vanished. Leaving Rhiannon undisturbed, they searched everywhere and failed to find the babe.

Fearful of being put to death when the Head of Annwn discovered their terrible fault, the women beat their brains, madly casting about for what best to do.

Then one of them said, 'The mother slept also while the child was taken. Let the fault be hers. I know of a stag-hound bitch that has just littered. If we kill some of her pups and smear Rhiannon's mouth and hands with their blood, and leave the bones scattered about her, surely it will be thought she has killed and eaten her own farrow.'

And that was what the women did.

Then with a great outcry they dragged Rhiannon awake, screaming how they had fought with her till they were covered in blood and bruises but had failed to prevent her from devouring her own innocent child.

Still blurred by weariness, Rhiannon woke at their noise. She saw the blood at her hands and the small bones lying beside her. Then in a trance of incomprehension she put her hand to her mouth and felt the blood wet about her lips.

'Where is my baby?' she asked.

Again the women told her how they had struggled in vain to stop her tearing her own child limb from limb and eating it. Driven to distraction by the realization that her child was lost, unable to understand why the women were accusing her of so hideous a crime, Rhiannon begged them to tell her the truth.

When they said there was no other truth to tell her, Rhiannon began to scream for her lost child, beseeching the women not to bear false witness against her, even promising them her own protection if they were at fault and the truth was told. But the frightened women would give no other answer.

The atrocious news was brought to the Head of Annwn that his newborn child was dead at his wife's hands and that she had torn and eaten its flesh. The women showed him the little bones they had found, they made him gaze on the bloodstains smeared about Rhiannon's hands and lips. Crazed by grief, Pwyll heard his kinsmen demand that his Rhiannon be put away for her inhuman crime.

Then Pwyll asked his wife to speak for herself, and when he heard what she had to say – how she had wrapped her baby in his crib, then slept in exhaustion and woken to find herself in that terrible condition with no knowledge of what had become of her child and nothing in her heart but inconsolable grief at its loss – he wanted to believe her.

'You had cause to ask me to put my wife away when she had no offspring,' he told his kinsmen, 'but I know her to have a child, though I cannot tell what has become of him. I will not put her away.'

Still they argued with him, saying that his unreasoning love for his wife had clouded his judgement. One by one the women were made to swear again to the truth of their dreadful story. Again Pwyll was faced with the overwhelming evidence, and though he could find no answer for it, still he would not cut himself off entirely from Rhiannon.

'But if she has done wrong,' he said with a grieving heart, 'then let her do penance for it.'

So with nothing but her own unprovable truth to defend her against the lies of the women, the court found against Rhiannon and she was forced to do penance for a crime she had not committed. The judgement on her was that she must wait like a horse by the mounting-block outside the gate at Arberth for the space of seven years and offer to carry every stranger on her back from the gate to the court. Pwyll could commute this sentence only in so far as he insisted that Rhiannon first be allowed to tell her story to each stranger that came.

Resigned to passing her stricken life that way as any other, Rhiannon took up her post at the gate; but though many travellers came that way, it is said that after listening to her moving story few had the heart to add their own weight to her already grievous burdens.

In those days the lord of Gwent Is-Coed was a generous hearted man called Teyrnon. Though his wife had not been able to give him an heir, he loved her nonetheless and consoled himself for the sadness with the satisfaction he took in his reputation as a notable breeder of horses. He kept in his stable a brood mare that all agreed was the finest in the land. Around the time Pwyll married Rhiannon, Teyrnon put the mare to his stallion and eagerly anticipated a further fine addition to his stock.

The mare was expected to foal on May Eve, yet when Teyrnon went into her stable at first light he found the mare had cast but there was no sign of the foal. After angry searching and suspicious enquiry round the neighbourhood failed either to find a newborn foal or account for its disappearance, the bitterly disappointed man resolved to try the mare again the following year. Again she was expected to foal on May Eve; again to Teyrnon's dismay no foal was dropped.

By May Eve of the next year Teyrnon was determined either to save the new foal or discover what mysterious fate befell it, so he told his wife that he intended to watch over the mare throughout the night. With his sword beside him, he sat with the mare among the straw, tending her as she laboured and watching as, eventually in the small hours of that moonless night, she cast a fine, handsome foal almost as large as a colt. Instantly it stood up on its gawky legs and staggered about in the straw.

Teyrnon saw at once that here was a champion among foals. He got to his feet, beaming with delight as he stood back to admire the sturdy way the colt turned to its mother for suck. At that moment he heard an outlandish din in the yard outside, then the window-shutter banged open and a huge shining arm was thrust through into the stable. Its taloned hand grabbed the foal by the mane and was dragging it helplessly towards the door when Teyrnon recovered his wits, snatched up his sword, and hacked through the arm till it released its grip on the foal and fell off in the bloody straw. The night filled with hideous screaming. Teyrnon pulled open the door and ran out into the yard after the noise, but he could see nothing in the blackness of the night. Then he heard a wailing at his back. Remembering he had left the door open, he turned quickly on his heel, ran back inside, and there beside the foal among the straw he found a newborn infant wrapped in a mantle of silk.

Examining the baby in amazement, Teyrnon saw that it was a boy and unusually strong and sturdy for its tender age. Gathering it up at once, he rushed into his wife, waking her with his shouts, and telling her that he had brought her the son that they had both desired for so long. Bemused by his shouts, his wife woke from her sleep to find the child thrust into her arms.

'But these garments,' she said, after the first flush of astonishment had passed, 'they are of the finest brocaded silk. Surely this is a well-born child. Its parents must be people of noble birth.' Then, struggling with her own needs and hopes, she asked her husband to tell her again how he had found the child.

'Surely the babe must be destined for our care,' he ended.

'There are women about me who love me,' his wife said after a time. 'If I asked it of them they would swear I have been with child.'

'Then none could dispute our claim to the boy,' said Teyrnon.

So out of the love and need of their hearts, husband and wife conspired together to raise the child as their own. When a shining nimbus of hair appeared on the boy's head they named him Gwri Wallt Euryn, Gwri of the Golden Hair.

Not long afterwards news came of the terrible fate that had be-fallen Rhiannon. Anxiously aware of his own good fortune in finding Gwri around the time when Rhiannon's child had disappeared, Teyrnon cautiously enquired into the matter. But when judgement was found against Rhiannon and she was put to her penance, he decided that the matter was settled, and relaxed into the joyful business of bringing up his son.

Before he was a year old the prodigious child was on his feet, bigger than a three-year-old, and walking as sturdily.

By the time he was two he had the stature of a six-year-old, and before he was five he was pestering the grooms to let him lead the horses to the water.

So great was the child's love for horses, Teyrnon soon decided that the colt born in the hour that he had found the child should be carefully broken in as Gwri's own mount. Then the happiness of all in Gwent Is-coed seemed complete.

Yet the more the boy grew, the more both parents were struck by his resemblance to Pwyll the Head of Annwyn. For a time they could not bring themselves to talk about it, but when Pwyll came on a progress through those parts and they saw how haggard he was, and when they thought of Rhiannon's continuing affliction at the gate of Arberth, the knowledge pained their honest hearts. At last Teyrnon could bear the anxiety no longer.

'Have you seen how much Gwri resembles Pwyll?' he asked his wife.' And when she admitted that she had observed it, he said, 'And do you recall that Gwri came to us at the same time that Rhiannon lost her child?' Again his wife nodded. 'Then it cannot be right,' Teyrnon said, 'for us to keep the son of the Head of Annwyn as our own while he mourns the loss, and as good a lady as Rhiannon suffers so grievously for it.'

With scarcely endurable sadness his wife agreed that they must deliver up the boy in the hope of thanks for the care they had given him, and with the thought that the grateful Head of Annwn might allow Teyrnon to act as the boy's foster father.

So they went with Gwri to Arberth and found Rhiannon waiting at the mounting-block by the gate. When she told them her sad story and offered to take them on her back, Gwri himself was the first to refuse out of pity for her condition. Then Teyrnon said that he and his wife hoped to free her from her burdens not to add to them, and bade her come to the court with them.

Pwyll himself had just returned from his progress around Dyfed and was surprised to find his presence demanded so soon in counsel. When he came into the hall he found his druid, Pendaran Dyfed, standing among the noblemen beside Rhiannon, and across from them the celebrated horse breeder, Teyrnon, lord of Gwent Is-coed, together with his wife and a tall golden haired child who strangely resembled Pwyll himself.

Then Teyrnon told the whole story of how he had found the boy and raised him as his own, yet had come to believe with increasing anguish that Gwri must be the lost son of Pwyll and Rhiannon.

'Believe me,' Rhiannon cried out, 'I should be delivered of my own anguish if that were true.'

'The truth of it is plain,' Pwyll cried joyfully. 'Look at the boy. Dare any in this whole company deny he is my son?'

Then the Head of Annwn called the boy across to him and they stood side by side, and so complete was the resemblance between them that none could dispute their kinship.

'What name did you give the boy?' the Druid Pendaran Dyfed asked Teyrnon.

'Gwri Golden Hair,' he was told.

'Yet I think his mother gave him his true name when she said that she was delivered of her anguish,' said the Druid; so ever afterwards the boy was known as Pryderi, which means 'anguish' in the tongue of Dyfed.

Yet there was no anguish and nothing but joy now in the court of the Head of Annwyn. Teyrnon and his wife were richly rewarded for the care they had lavished on the lost son of Rhiannon, and though the boy was given to be fostered by the druid Pendaran Dyfed, the honest couple were to remain his close companions and foster parents in matters of the heart.

So Pwyll, the Head of Annwyn, watched his son grow to manhood and before his own death he came to know him for the fairest and most accomplished leader of men in all the seven cantrefs of Dyfed.

7

The Children of Llyr

At the time when Britain was known as the Island of the Mighty, the Celtic peoples who lived there revered a great Goddess called Don. This goddess was the same Earth-mother, Danu, whose children were the *Tuatha de Danann* honoured by the Irish Gaels, and the 'Children of Don' were among the great ruling families of the British Gods.

That family found their shining places in the dome of the night sky above the Island of the Mighty. The constellation known to us as Cassiopeia's Chair was called *Llys Don* – Don's Court – by the Celts. The Northern Crown was known to them as *Caer Arianrhod* – the Castle of Don's Daughter, Arianrhod; and the Milky Way was *Caer Gwydion*, named for one of Don's sons. But the greatest of her sons was Nudd, who was called *Llaw Ereint*, 'the Silver-Handed', a name which reveals him as the British counterpart of Nuada Argetlam in the Irish myths, though no reason for the appellation survives in British lore.

Don also had another daughter called Penarddun, of whom little is known except that she was given in marriage to the great sea-god Llyr. In some of the stories that god is called *Llyr Llediath*, meaning Llyr of the Foreign Tongue, and he is evidently the same figure as the Irish sea-god, Lir.

Now the family of Don and the children of Llyr were often as fiercely in conflict as were the People of Danu and the sea-dwelling Fomorian giants in Ireland. So just as Brigid, the Dagda's daughter was wedded to Breas, son of the Fomorian Elathan; and Diancecht's son, Cian, married Balor's daughter, Eithne; so Penardunn was betrothed to Llyr in an attempt to heal the ancient wounds between the realms of sky and sea, between the powers of darkness and of light.

From this alliance were to spring three children.

A son called Manawydan was a great sea-dwelling magician who, like his Irish counterpart Manannan mac Lir, would willingly use his arts of enchantment for his friends, but was a terror to his enemies. It was he who built the bone fortress of Oeth and Anoeth in Gower, a massive labyrinthine prison-house constructed in the shape of a beehive out of human bones. Arthur himself was held captive there once.

By his wife Penardunn, Llyr fathered another son, Bran, and a daughter, Branwen. The beauty of Branwen of the Fair Bosom glittered like sunlight across the surface of the sea, while her noble brother Bran was built on such colossal scale that no house could hold him, nor was any ship large enough to take him aboard. Bran had an appetite for life as vast as his mighty body. He delighted as much in the carnage of warfare as did the raven from which he may have taken his name, but he was no less a great lover of feasting, merriment and song. A versatile poet and musician himself, he kept a special place in his huge heart for bards, who flourished under his open-handed patronage.

But Penarddun also had two other children, half-brothers to Bran and Branwen, by a man called Euroswydd. Of these two sons, one was amiable and peace loving while the other was constantly spoiling for trouble. Whenever a dispute broke out in the family, Nissyen would be at pains to end the conflict, speaking fairly with both quarrellers even at the height of their wrath. By contrast, with a kind of cold malignant revelry, his brother Evnissyen would tirelessly seek ways to stir up strife when everyone was most at peace.

Of the family of Llyr it was Bran who was crowned High King over the Isle of the Mighty, and though some say he was given that crown in *Caer Llundain*, he loved most to live on the wild shores of Wales, where he kept court on the castle-rock of Harddlech in Ardudwy overlooking the sea.

One day a fleet of thirteen ships was seen beating towards that coast from Ireland. Bran immediately ordered his guard to arms until the intentions of the foreigners came clear. Yet never had lovelier or more delicate vessels been seen along that coast, and when the lead ship fetched up closer inshore it was seen that it bore an inverted shield on its prow as a sign of peace. The great sail was dropped and a small boat put out from its side, bobbing its prow on the quiet swell. When it rode the breakers under the cliff within hailing distance of where Bran watched, the rowers shipped their oars.

Bidding the voyagers fair welcome, the king demanded to know whose fleet this was and why it had come to his shores.

'These ships belong to Matholwch, King of Ireland,' he was told, 'and he himself is here with them.'

'Then will he not come ashore?' Bran invited.

'By no means, except it be you grant what he is after.'

'And what might that be?'

'An alliance between Erin and the Island of the Mighty, that both might be the stronger for it.'

'A fair desire,' said Bran.

'There is more. Matholwch would seal that bond by asking for the hand in marriage of Branwen daughter of Llyr.'

'Then let him come ashore,' said Bran, 'and we will talk of these things together.'

So Matholwch came ashore, the two kings took counsel, and it was agreed quickly enough that the desirable alliance should be made and that Branwen would be given as wife to the Irish King at a great wedding feast to be celebrated at Aberffraw in Talebolion which is now called Anglesey.

Matholwch sailed to Talebolion with his fleet, while Bran and his retinue marched by land, bringing the bride with them in their garlanded train. Immense, airy pavilions were set up at Aberffraw, for there was no house large enough to contain Bran. At a banquet of unprecedented plenty, Branwen of the Fair Bosom became wife to the King of Ireland, and was known thereafter as one of the Three Matriarchs of the Island of the Mighty.

The feast itself was joyous enough and all things might have remained that way had it not been for the sinister malcontent, Evnissyen. Bran had not even informed his half-brother of the wedding, let alone consulted him about it, for he knew the man's perversity too well and the Irish alliance was far too valuable to risk any disruption of its progress. For the same prudent reason Evnissyen was not invited to the wedding.

At the end of that happy day Bran might have congratulated himself on the wisdom of the decision. Everything had passed off as happily as he could have wished. With much revelry and merriment, the bride and groom had been cheered off to the pleasures of their bed; and having drunk well and fed well to the sound of sweet music, the guests themselves – Britons and Irishmen together – nodded drunkenly towards slumber.

Meanwhile their servingmen sought billets for the horses in all the stables of the surrounding countryside. Attracted by the unusual night-time stamp of hooves, Evnissyen chanced upon one of these strings of horses. When he asked whom the splendid animals belonged to, he was proudly told they were the horses of Matholwch, King of Ireland.

Surprised by the reply he demanded to know what they were doing there by night.

'Have you not heard that the Irish King sleeps with Branwen of the Fair Bosom in Aberffraw,' he was answered, 'for they became husband and wife this day in celebration of a grand alliance that is made between Bran and himself?'

Stunned by the news, Evnissyen allowed the thought of Bran's insult to fester in his brain till it conceived a revenge that might swiftly undo all the good that had been done that day.

Under cover of darkness he entered the stable taking a sharp knife with him, and there he set about mutilating the King of Ireland's horses. Amidst terrible screams, he cut their lips to the teeth, their ears from their heads, the tails from their haunches.

Where his free hand could get at them he even sliced off the soft lids of their eyes. Then he left the poor beasts, maimed and useless in the bloody straw, for the grooms to find and bring word to the King of Ireland about the manner in which Bran had stabled them.

Matholwch's rage at the news was matched only by his horror. His counsellors said that such a terrible thing could never have been done without Bran's consent, and that no worse insult had ever been inflicted on an Irish king. Unable to comprehend how Bran could have done him such injury after giving him his own fair sister in marriage, Matholwch strove for clarity, yet the vileness of the deed and the urgings of his kinsmen left him aflame with thoughts of vengeance.

Bran woke that morning to the bewildering news that the Irishmen were breaking camp and making for their ships. Immediately he sent messengers to discover the cause, but by the time they returned with the news of Matholwch's injured fury, Bran had already learned from Evnissyen's own remorseless lips the dreadful harm that had been done.

Word was brought to Matholwch that the malefactor had been found and the Irish King's immediate demand was for his death. Then Bran was forced to explain that it would be hard for him to kill Evnissyen because he was his own half-brother on his mother's side, a man driven from birth by his disfigured mind. Unable to take on the blood-guilt of a kinsman's death, Bran offered instead to replace every horse that was lost and, in further atonement, he would make additional precious gifts to Matholwch of a golden plate as round as his face and a silver staff as tall as the Irish King himself.

Matholwch took counsel with his men and found their opinion divided. Yet with his first fury cooled, and measuring his own present strength against that of the Island of the Mighty, he calculated that it would be wiser to accept Bran's offer than to reject it. To Branwen's great relief the rift was avoided.

So the fair pavilions were pitched again, and a banquet of reconciliation was arranged. Yet the mood of the marriage-feast had darkened, and it was hard for Matholwch to speak fondly with his brother-in-law while the thought of what had been done to his horses still rankled in his heart.

Troubled by his taciturn frown, Bran decided that further reparation must be made. With a generosity that astonished even those who knew him best, Bran offered his sister's husband no less a prize than the magic Cauldron of Regeneration. It had been brought to the Island of the Mighty out of the deeps of an Irish lake in ancient times, and had the property of restoring all signs of life to any dead man placed inside it, save only that he would lack the power of speech. In order that any ill feeling between Matholwch and himself should vanish once and for all, Bran restored the vessel to the king of the land whence it had come.

With a gladdened heart, Matholwch accepted the prodigious gift, forgiving all injury he had taken at the hands of Evnissyen. At the end of the renewed festivities he and Branwen happily boarded ship and made sail for Ireland.

All the great Irish princes and their wives assembled to welcome their new queen. There was not one among them to whom Branwen did not give some precious gift — a ring, a brooch, a torque or precious gemstone out of her own treasury. Her generous heart won great acclaim and when, within a year, Branwen had given birth to a fine son called Gwern, it might have seemed that his joyous birth had crowned and blessed the union of two great kingdoms. Yet not long afterwards evil took root in the high court of Ireland.

On his return from the Island of the Mighty, Matholwch had made no mention of the terrible mutilation of his horses. The harm had been done by a malcontent and made good by a friend, and he thought that nothing but trouble could come from raking over those coals in the company of hot-headed men, some of whom had resented the foreign marriage.

Yet truth will not be concealed for ever and when Matholwch's foster brothers learned how readily their king had settled for compensation, they despised him for it. In their opinion the insult was so hideous that Matholwch should have taken vengeance on the malefactor first, and then demanded reparation. They thought it base scorn that he had not done so, and were not slow or quiet in mouthing that opinion.

Now it is hard for a proud king to live with the knowledge that his own kinsmen are murmuring against him. Harder still when there lurks in his mind the thought that they might be in the right of it. Soon what had once seemed an enterprise of great skill and hope – his sound diplomacy, the happy marriage that sealed it, the forgiveness of injury and the rich rewards it brought – all turned, in Matholwch's darkened mind, to a history of disgrace and shame. The joy he had once taken in his wife's company shrivelled in the dull heat of his suppressed rage. Then that rage was out of him at last, and it was Branwen that was made to suffer for it.

Watching the king's mood turn against her, his kinsmen heaped ever harsher insults on her innocent, astonished head. When Branwen looked to Matholwch for help, she met black fury there. Further angered by her reproach, he turned her out of his chamber. The unhappy woman's misery was increased when she saw her infant son sent away to be fostered by a stern lord of the clan. At last, alone and humiliated, with not a single friend around her, and no one to plead her cause, Branwen was put to work among the scullions in the hot kitchen where each morning the bloody-handed butcher took it on himself to give her clouts about the head.

Knowing what vengeance Bran was likely to take if word reached him of her dishonouring, Matholwch put a stop to all traffic between Ireland and the Island of the Mighty. So Branwen suffered three years of affliction in the kitchen of the Irish court, taking no scrap of comfort there except that which came from caring for an injured starling she found by the kneading-trough one day. Recognizing another victim of wanton cruelty, she fed the bird morsels at her own hand, and gave it water to drink till it was strong enough to take flight again. After that the starling came tamely to her call, and at each tender visit it brought a tiny glint of hope.

In such quiet time as was left to her, Branwen would sit with the bird perched at her shoulder or on her finger, teaching the starling to speak Bran's name, and telling it what manner of man her brother was and where he might be found. When she was sure the starling understood what was asked of it, she made shift to find a scrap of paper on which she wrote a letter telling Bran of her plight. Fixing the folded paper by a ring to the starling's leg, Branwen lifted the bird in her two hands and lofted it skywards, praying that its windy flight across the sea would bring the message safely to her brother.

Bran the Blessed was sitting in counsel in Arfon one day when a bird flew into the hall, fluttered about his head, and then alighted on his shoulder. His counsellors laughed when they heard it speak his name, calling it a sign of good omen. As the starling ruffled and preened its feathers someone observed the glint of sunlight from the ring at its leg. 'This bird has been reared among men,' he said, gently taking it in his hand. Then he saw the paper tucked behind the ring. As soon as the paper was unfolded and the message read, Bran's huge heart tore open between rage at what Matholwch had done to his sister, and grief for her pitiful condition.

Messengers were immediately dispatched across the Island of the Mighty, summoning all its great princes to a council of war. Bran addressed the assembly himself, and his passionate account of Branwen's sufferings at Matholwch's false hands worked powerfully on the prince's hearts. It was quickly decided that all but seven of them would follow Bran to Ireland. The others were appointed to watch over the kingdom under the regency of Bran's son, Cradawg.

In those days the deep water between Erin and the Island of the Mighty was not wide, so Bran – who was, it will be remembered, too huge for any ship to carry him – waded across Manawydan's meadows with the masts of his great fleet crowded about him.

No one in Ireland had got wind of their coming. Thus when two of Matholwch's swineherds who had let their pigs forage on the shore that day looked out to sea they saw a sight so strange their eyes could make no sense of it. Rushing back to Matholwch's court, they brought a confused account of how they had seen a thick forest growing on the surface of the sea, and near it a high mountain with a steep ridge near its crest and a lake on either side of that ridge. No such things had been seen in that place before, they said, yet the true terror of it was that forest, mountain, ridge and lakes were all on the move.

Matholwch turned in bewilderment to his counsellors but none of them could read these signs. Then someone suggested that if these things were coming over the water from the Island of the Mighty then Branwen might explain the mystery of it. So Branwen was brought out of the kitchen and when she was told what the swineherds had seen she uttered a fierce laugh.

'What is the forest that was seen on the sea?' Matholwch demanded.

'It is the masts and yards of the ships bearing the army of the Island of the Mighty,' she answered him triumphantly.

'Then what is the mountain with the two lakes at its ridge?'

'What else but the head of my brother Bran the Blessed wading through the sea,' Branwen answered. 'The ridge is his nose, and the lakes at either side of it are his two eyes. And he is come here in his rage, having heard of my woes and humiliation.'

A panicked war council was immediately called, but the leaders could think of no better plan than to withdraw all their troops across the River Llinon, breaking the bridge behind them. So they beat their retreat and once the river was crossed, Matholwch ordered the bridge pulled down and watched as its stones were thrown into the deeps of the river.

When Bran's scouts came ashore they could find no way for the army to come at their enemies. The baffled warriors turned for counsel to Bran, who said, 'Is it not the work of a leader to be a bridge among men? I will lay my own body down as a bridge across the river. You shall cross by me.'

Watching Bran stretch his colossal frame across the Llinon, and his men fetching hurdles so that the whole army could pass over him in safety, the Irishmen knew there was no hope against such power. Thus it was that when Bran got back to his feet he found Matholwch's heralds already waiting for him. Their message was plain and unconditional. In the interests of immediate peace, and as reparation for the great wrong that had been done to Branwen, Matholwch would put his own person at Bran's mercy, resigning the throne of Ireland in favour of his son Gwern, who was Branwen's child, and close kin to Bran himself.

But Bran was not to be appeased so easily.

'And what if I should want the kingdom for myself?' he said. 'How would you stop me taking it? Go back to your false king. Tell him he will have no word from me again until he makes a larger offer.'

Daunted by this implacable message, Matholwch gathered his counsellors about him once more. One of them suggested that nothing might better please Bran than if they built an immense palace for him because there had never been a house large enough for him to enter before. When this was agreed, another cunningly suggested that it might be wise to construct that palace in such a way that an army might be concealed inside it. So the heralds returned offering the kingship of Ireland to Bran together with a newly built royal palace roomy enough to shelter him and both his hosts – the one he brought with him, and the one waiting to serve him as the new king.

When Bran asked his sister about her feelings on the matter, Branwen said that for all her sufferings she had no wish to see the land laid waste; so Bran accepted the kingship of Ireland on these terms.

The day came when the vast coronation hall was completed, but before Bran came to stand beneath a roof for the first time in his life, his half-brother Evnissyen, whose perverse heart lay at the root of all these troubles, entered the hall alone to look it over.

It wasn't long before his cunning gaze fell on the hide-sacks which hung, strangely bulky, from thick pegs on either side of each of the hundred pillars holding up the roof.

Going up to one of them, he asked what was in the sack.

'Flour,' he was told.

Nodding, Evnissyen put his hand into the neck of the sack as though to sift the flour; then between finger and thumb he squeezed the head of the warrior hidden there until the man's brains were out. Passing on to the next sack, he asked what it contained. 'Flour, friend,' he was told again. Again he put his hand to the sack and kneaded the head of the warrior within till he had squashed it. Smiling, Evnissyen passed from pillar to pillar of the hall that way and not one of the warriors hidden there came out of his sack alive. Then that creature of the shadows made a song about the soft, lumpy flour of Ireland, and bade his half-brother Bran enter the hall.

Bran and the host of the Island of the Mighty came into the hall from one side of the fire burning on the broad hearth beneath the central chimney, and the Irish host entered with their defeated king from the other. Matholwch yielded up all the royal regalia of his kingship to Bran, and a treaty of peace was concluded between the kingdoms. Then, to the great joy of all, rather than taking the crown of Ireland for himself Bran conferred it on his half-Irish grandson Gwern, to whom it now rightfully belonged.

When the solemnities of Gwern's consecration were over, Branwen's delightful child ran gaily from Bran's tender embrace to greet his adoring uncle Manawydan. From there he passed happily into the hug of Bran's good-natured half-brother, Nissyen; and all three played with the boy and felt their hearts leap with love for the infant king.

After a time, from the place where he had watched these fond embraces, Evnissyen spoke out. 'Why does my half-sister's son not come to me? Even if he were not king of all Ireland I would still wish to show him the strength of my love.'

After a moment's hesitation in which he caught Branwen's anxious glance, Bran smiled and said, 'Let the boy go to him.'

Evnissyen too was smiling as Gwern ran happily towards him, but the secret cause of his smile was the sudden knowledge that he was about to do something so terrible that no one there could even conceive of it. When Gwern reached him, he lifted the boy high up in his arms, laughed loudly at his innocent, responsive chuckle, and then – before anyone realized what was about to happen – he tossed the child into the blazing fire.

Gwern's shining hair instantly flared into a torch. The fire wrapped him as swiftly in a cape of flame, and so fierce was the heat in that huge hearth that the burning child could not climb out of it nor could any man reach in to save him.

In the paralyzed silence of the hall Evnissyen stared at the small combusting body as if stupefied by the enormity of his own atrocious deed. When her own eyes took in what had been done to her child, Branwen became a single, unceasing scream. Impelled by its own power, that scream would have hurled her into the blaze after her son had not Bran quickly pulled her back. Then, as if suddenly taking flame itself, the silence all around Branwen's frantic screaming crackled into cries of treason, and every man was reaching for his sword.

Dragging Branwen from the sight of her son and beyond reach of the flashing blades, Bran held his crazed sister between his shoulder and his shield and carried her out of that calamitous place.

Then blood was everywhere. So many warriors were packed together in that space that no such butchery was ever seen inside a house before. It became a palace of exterminations.

Day after day the killing went on. The Irishmen lit a fire under the Cauldron of Regeneration that Bran had given back to them. Each night they plunged the bodies of their fallen warriors inside it. Each dawn the Irish dead rose out of the vat alive to resume the fight in fearsome silence. But the warriors of the Island of the Mighty had no magical means to make good their losses. Unstoppably their numbers dwindled, and when Evnissyen saw the bodies of his kinsmen piled about him in that dreadful place, for the first time in the cruel history of his invert heart a crack of feeling entered. He experienced it as the lacerations of remorse.

'My life will be a curse for ever now,' he thought, 'if I can find no way to end the guilt of it.'

So he fought his way through the tumult till he came to the place near the cauldron where the dead Irishmen were stacked. There he covered his body with an Irish robe, and lay down lax among them.

When the sweating workers at the cauldron came by dark to lift him up, Evnissyen lay, eyes closed, unbreathing, and let them topple him over the enchanted rim. Once among the dark boil of limbs inside the cauldron, he strained every muscle in an immense effort of concentrated power to swell the girth of his body wider and still wider till it burst the iron sides of the cauldron apart and his own heart with it.

With the shattering of the cauldron, the battle turned against the Irishmen till the last of them lay dead in his blood. It is said that after the bloodshed of that time, there was no one left alive among the Irish people except five pregnant women who hid themselves in a cave in the wilderness, and it was by the sons they bore that the five provinces of Ireland were founded. Yet the cost to the Island of the Mighty was more terrible than any could have dreamed when they set out on this cruel war. Of all the proud host who had entered the hall with Bran, only seven escaped from it alive. They were Pryderi, Manawydan, Gluneu, Ynawc, Grudyen son of Muryel, Heilyen son of Gwynn the Ancient, and Taliesin the Bard.

Bran himself had been wounded in the foot by a poisoned spear that gave him intolerable pain. Nor was even his mighty heart large enough to contain the suffering that had come upon his people. His only desire now was for death; so he called his surviving lords together and bade them cut off his head and take it for burial to the White Mount in Caer Llundain.

Yet before the head was struck from his body he prophesied how their journey would bring them to Harddlech, where they would hear the singing of the birds of Rhiannon which could sing the dead to life and enrapture the living in the sleep of death. After feasting there for seven years they would come to the Isle of Gwales where during four-score years of further feasting they would be so enchanted by the entertaining conversation of his own uncorrupted head that they would forget the flight of time. The seven would remain in that place until one of them opened the door which looked towards Cornwall, then time would capture them again, and they would hasten to Caer Llundain where they would bury his head at last on the White Mount, gazing towards France.

So in great wonderment and grief of heart, the seven did as Bran bade them and severed his noble head from its vast body.

Then, bringing Branwen with them, they tenderly laid the head in a ship and made sail for the Island of the Mighty.

The ship made landfall first at Aber Alaw in the island of Talebolion. From that shining estuary Branwen gazed for the last time back towards Ireland. Turning her head, she looked to where the Island of the Mighty gleamed in the haze across the strait. 'Alas that ever I was born,' she cried, 'for two great islands are laid waste because of me.'

Even the sea birds in the brakes were silenced by the grief of that cry, and in that hush was heard the breaking of Branwen's heart. There on the banks of the Alaw they buried the body of the fairest queen that was ever seen in either Erin or the Island of the Mighty, and the four-sided mound they raised over her would ever afterwards be known as *Ynys Branwen*.

The remnant of Bran's host made their grieving way towards Harddlech then, bringing the noble head with them. From a band of travellers they learned that treason had been at work during their absence from the Island of the Mighty. While wearing a mantle of invisibility, Caswallawn – one of the seven lords left to guard the Island – had murdered six of his colleagues before crowning himself king in Caer Llundain. When Manawydan demanded to know what had become of his nephew, Cradawg, he was told that Caswallawn would have spared the life of Bran's son as a kinsman, but Cradawg had not been able to bear the sorrow of losing his father's kingdom and had died from it.

Burdened by this further news of disaster, the seven entered Harddlech then and sat down at its great table to refresh themselves. As they ate and drank, the air about their heads thrilled to the sounds of music sweeter and more deeply stirring than any of them had heard before. Looking for the source of this rapturous enchantment, they saw three birds gliding far out over the sea, yet their song carried so clearly across the ocean air, the birds might have been singing at their shoulders in the hall. It was the birds of Rhiannon that moved their souls as Bran had foretold they would, and so exquisite was the music they made that all the songs loved by the seven before that time now seemed unlovely to their ears.

The days became weeks and the weeks years as they feasted at Harddlech under the sweet spell of that music. At the end of the seventh year the birds at last took flight. Bringing Bran's still uncorrupted head along with them, the seven lords made their way to Gwales, and when they arrived at that island they found a royal house waiting for them on a headland overlooking the sea. Inside its splendid hall were three doors, two of which stood open for them to pass through as they wished, but the third was firmly closed.

'See,' Manawydan said, 'that is the door we must not open if we would keep time at bay.'

Tenderly they uncovered Bran's noble head and set it down where a feast was prepared for them. As they began to eat, Bran's eyes opened and smiled at them, and the voice they knew and loved so well gave them fair welcome. And on that instant it was as if time stood still and all the loss and grief and sorrow they had known took flight from their hearts, leaving only a blessed sense of peace and contentment and increasing joy as they remembered how Bran had promised them many years of pleasant conversation in that place.

And so it transpired, for if Bran had been wise and eloquent and full of stirring poetry in the time before he had gone to Ireland, such transporting powers were as nothing compared with the words that flowed from the enchanted imagination of his severed head. For every thought that he uttered was filled with the intelligence of the heart, and for every question they put to him he had an answer drawn from realms beyond the experience of those who had not yet tasted death, yet which spoke to them with quiet certainties that ravished their hearts and minds. And just as time was banished by the joyous entertaining of the noble head, so too its fluent, tranquil words dispelled all memory of the world which they had left behind and of the cares that waited for them there.

Though fourscore years unfolded across time outside that palace, no sign of ageing was to be seen about the limbs and faces of the enraptured seven as they feasted round Bran's venerable head, and talked with it long and heartily without knowing a moment's tedium in all that gap of time.

Yet a day came – perhaps at the silent, knowing bidding of the head itself – when Heilyn, son of Gwynn the Ancient, rose to his feet from the great table, vowing that he would know once and for all whether or not it was true what was said about the closed door. Putting his hand to the latch, he threw the door open and found himself looking out where sunlight broke across the rugged coast of Cornwall. In that same instant the enchantment failed. Like a sudden brusque wind, the memory of all the sorrows they had known rushed in on them – the burning of Gwern, the killing of their kinsmen and friends, the breaking of Branwen's injured heart, the murder of the six lords by Caswallawn, and how the young regent Cradawg had died for the loss of his father's land. The pain of it all overwhelmed each one of them, and weeping till they had no more tears to shed they grieved for the death of their lord as if they had suffered that bereavement no more than an hour before.

Thereafter their hearts would give them no peace till they had carried Bran's silent, decaying head to Caer Llundain where, as he had bidden them in Ireland long before, they buried it beneath the White Mount with its face gazing towards France. Because it was to lie there undisturbed for many centuries protecting the Island of the Mighty from invasion, that burial was known as one of Three Happy Concealments. Yet a time would come when the venerable head was disinterred, and that was one of the Three Calamitous Uncoverings of Britain. For in proud quest of his own destiny, and thinking it base scorn to hold the island other than by valour, Arthur would have the head of Bran dug up again. Not long thereafter the Island of the Mighty fell in thraldom to the English and the Saxon hordes.

8

The War of Enchantments

With the passing of Bran, Manawydan was the last of Llyr's children left alive. Bran's heir Cradawg had died when the traitor Caswallawn deposed him as regent and seized the throne, so kingship over the Island of the Mighty should now rightfully have passed from Bran to Manawydan. Yet Manawydan had been left homeless and landless by the years of wandering and was in no position to bid for his throne. Thus, in the absence of opposition after the terrible losses suffered by the loyal host in Ireland, Caswallawn was able to consolidate his rule.

After the burial of Bran's head, Manawydan's friends did their best to console him for the wretchedness of his situation. The case was not without hope, they said. Was not Manawydan famous as one of the Three Selfless Chieftains of the land? They felt sure that if he sought a place at court, then his cousin Caswallawn would surely grant it. But Manawydan was too proud to entreat such patronage, nor could he live happily in a house where a traitor sat in Bran's place, so it seemed he was destined to a life of exile and insecurity. Then aid came to him from a different quarter.

After the death of Pwyll Head of Annwn, his son Pryderi became King of Dyfed, and gained yet more lands by his marriage to Cigva, daughter of Gwyn Gloyw. Though all his estates were held under homage to Caswallawn as High King of the Island of the Mighty, Pryderi had no great love for the usurper, and it was he who offered refuge to Manawydan in Dyfed now. Since they had first met, warm bonds of affection had grown between the older and the younger man. To make them still stronger Pryderi suggested that a marriage might be arranged between Manawydan and his widowed mother, Rhiannon.

'In all your wanderings you can have met no wiser woman, nor one of fairer speech,' Pryderi said; 'and though the years have come upon her she is beautiful to look on. It would gladden my heart if the two of you were to wed and govern the seven cantrefs for me.'

Heartened and moved by his young friend's generosity, Manawydan happily agreed to travel to Dyfed with him. A great feast was prepared for their arrival at Arberth, and at the earliest opportunity Pryderi drew aside with his wife, Cigva, leaving Manawydan and Rhiannon alone to talk together. For a long time the two ageing people shared stories of the joys and sorrows of their adventurous lives and the wisdom they had learned from them. Soon Manawydan felt his heart stirring with love for a woman who had so nobly endured so much, and Rhiannon was amazed to find herself quickening once more to the sensitive attention of a wise and courageous man.

When Pryderi and Cigva eventually interrupted their long conversation with a light remark, Manawydan smiled and said, 'Pryderi, it would please me dearly to take you at your word!'

'What word was that?' asked Rhiannon.

Then Pryderi told his mother that he had long wanted to ease the loneliness she had felt since his father's death. If she could learn to care for Manawydan as much as he loved the man himself, he said, then it was his wish that a marriage might be made between his mother and his friend.

With the breath arrested at his throat Manawydan waited for her response. There was a moment's thoughtful silence; then, as if no possible destiny could have come closer to her own desires, Rhiannon happily assented to her son's wish.

She took Manawydan to her bed that night, and both of them found such tenderness there as neither of them had thought to know again.

The next day Pryderi decided to delay the journey on which he would pay homage to Caswallawn so that the feasting could continue unabated. The two couples passed a happy time progressing across the beautiful hunting country of Dyfed and deepening the bonds of love between them. But on their return to Arberth, Pryderi could postpone his embassy no longer. Leaving his wife in the care of his mother and his friend, he set out to do his act of homage at the court of the High King.

Anxious to forestall possible trouble from Dyfed, Caswallawn received his vassal cordially enough, even asking after Manawydan's health and wishing him well. Then he pressed Pryderi to stay with him for a time in a manner that could not be easily refused. But the young Prince of Dyfed was ill at ease in the tense, extravagant life of that court where shifts of power and favour were all the talk and people's minds were sharper than their hearts were warm. Though he was lionized there, and gratified by the attention, Pryderi missed the simple contentment of his life in Dyfed – the elation of urging a mettlesome horse across the lovely rigour of its landscapes, and the wild music of its wind and sea. Above all he longed for the uncomplicated love of his wife and friends, the joy they took in one another's company, the laughter, the poetry, the deep true conversations that unfolded between them in Arberth as the harvest of experience.

As soon as he could graciously do so, Pryderi took leave of the King and his arid, excitable court, and hastened back to the life and people he loved. Messengers rode ahead and when he arrived a huge feast among his friends was waiting for him. When it was over he progressed with the certainty of a man who knows his life sane and whole, to the soft loving welcome of his wife's bed.

On Pryderi's return, the pattern of life at Arberth resumed and renewed itself, for the horses seemed more spirited after his absence, the food still more wholesome, the music more haunting, and his friends incomparably the best company in the world. Nothing was lacking for their contentment.

One evening while they were feasting at the hall, the conversation turned to the magical mound outside Arberth where Pwyll had first set eyes on Rhiannon. Stirred once more by the old story, and heady with wine, Pryderi insisted that the time had surely come when he too should experience the mystery of the mound. So leaving the rest of that festive company, he and Cigva went out into the fresh night air accompanied only by Manawydan and Rhiannon.

The dwindling moon of a star-bright sky cast a thin milky light over the pastures where the cattle grazed. They could still faintly hear the revelry of the feast around the hearths in Arberth as the four of them climbed the mound together and sat down wondering whether blows or marvels lay in wait for them.

Instantly a pang of lightning seared the night, followed by the close unrolling of thunder. Then a dense mist came driving in towards them, thickening the air and hiding them from one another in its drapes. Alarmed, they all got to their feet and were about to call out through that sudden isolating gloom, but even as their mouths opened to shape their cries the mist dispersed as quickly as it had come and they were caught in the glare of a harsh exposing light.

When they were able to open their eyes again they were looking out not across the abundant moonlit meadows of Arberth but on a barren waste. The herds and flocks that had been grazing around them only moments before had all vanished, the air was murky and still, smokeless for the want of the fires that had been burning in the hearths of the court when they left. The buildings themselves seemed derelict and silent. Nowhere was there any sign of life.

Manawydan was the first to speak the dismay they all felt at that sudden desolating change. 'What has happened?' he said. 'Where is the great company that was in the hall?' And when none answered him : 'We should go back and look for them.'

But when, with anxious hearts, they entered the hall at Arberth they found it as empty and silent as it had seemed from the distance of the mound. No hounds bounded to greet them, none of the familiar servants were there anticipating need, no friends rose laughing to ask after their adventure. Not even a wren stirred among the beams of the roof. Together and singly, they passed from chamber to deserted chamber, calling as they went, yet heard no warmer answer than the echoes of their own cries in the gloom. Evidently a great company had once feasted there, but where they had gone, and why, were questions that resisted answer; and that feast itself might have happened a century or more ago.

When the four of them assembled again by the cold hearth in the hall, they could only stare at each other for a time as if contaminated by the silence of the place.

The night passed, then a day and another night, and still they saw no one. By then they had searched their minds and hearts to explain the evil mystery of the thing but to no avail. It seemed only that Manawydan must be right in his conviction that, for reasons they did not understand, the enchantment of the mound had somehow been turned against them. And by now there was a closer problem: they had eaten what food they had foraged from about the hall and their hunger was growing.

'There will be deer and fowl in the wilderness about us, and fish in its streams, and honey from the wild bees' said Pryderi. 'Though we have no friends to share our pleasures, we have the comfort of each other still, and the joy of the hunt is waiting for us.'

So for a time they lived as hunters in the wild, preferring to sleep under the open sky of Dyfed rather than be reminded by the desolate hall of all that was now lost to them. Yet it was hard to bear the lack of the gracious society that had always been about them in Arberth; and dearly though they cared for each other, increasingly they felt the want of a world around them. It was Manawydan who made them face this at last.

'Dear friends,' he said, 'in this strangely altered state where the world we knew is taken from us, you have comforted me and cheered my spirits and lifted up my heart so that I have felt at times almost as I did with my six companions in Gwales listening to the marvellous entertainment of Bran's head. Yet a time came there when the door was opened and the entertainment was at an end and all our forgotten sorrows were borne back in on us. I think that we too have now come to such a time. We cannot live alone like this much longer and still keep good company. I think we must make some alteration in our lives.'

When Pryderi asked what his friend proposed, Manawydan pointed out that as long as they lived like creatures of the wild, foraging for survival, they were yielding up all power to whoever it was that had worked this enchantment against them. The time had come for them to venture back into the world and see what destiny unfolded for them there.

'But we have no revenues,' Pryderi protested, 'no way of keeping food in our mouths there, or clothes on our backs.'

'Then we must learn new skills,' said Manawydan, 'I have a trick or two about me that may see us through.'

So under his guidance and leadership the four friends came to the city of Hereford in Caswallawn's lands in Lloegyr, and there Manawydan quickly established a successful saddlery, making pommels and saddles of the highest quality, and colouring the leather with a technique he had learned long before from a craftsman skilled in the use of blue-azure. So beautiful was their workmanship that they began to put the established saddlers out of business, and it wasn't long before their rivals conspired against the newcomers.

When the disgruntled tradesmen threatened them with violence, Pryderi was all for fighting, but Manawydan insisted that no good could come of that when their own numbers were so small. There was nothing for it, he said, but to move on to another town.

'How shall we get our living there?' Pryderi demanded.

'We will make shields,' said Manawydan.

'Do we know anything about that?'

'We can learn,' Manawydan answered. And thinking of the shields that had best served him in his fighting days, he set to work and soon they were producing the strongest and most beautiful shields in the town. The business prospered and once more jealous competitors made trouble for them. Again Pryderi wanted to fight; again Manawydan counselled prudent flight. So they moved on to another town where they set up as cordwainers, with Manawydan shaping the shoes while Pryderi stitched them. They befriended a master goldsmith who furnished them with splendid buckles that drew still more buyers for their wares, and once more it wasn't long before the success of their enterprise left them victim to angry rivals.

By now Pryderi had wearied of the craftsman's way of life. His proud spirit was that of a prince and a lover of horses. He felt cramped and humiliated in the narrow workshops among the noisy, grasping crowds that seemed always to have an eye only for the main chance. His heart ached for the wild horse-country of his own domains however desolate they now were.

So gathering his friends together he insisted that their time in the wilderness of Dyfed might have been less prosperous but it was far happier than the years they had wasted among the troublesome throng of the towns in Lloegyr. To his mind, if they were not strong enough to stand and fight against those who meant them harm, then they should return to the place they loved best and make a life there as well as they could.

Manawydan was less certain of the wisdom of this course but when he saw that Cigva and Rhiannon shared Pryderi's feelings, he was persuaded to sell the business, buy a pack of hounds with the profits and go back with them into the wilds.

They had been living in Dyfed for some months when Pryderi and Manawydan went out hunting one morning and saw their hounds pull back from an encounter in a thick copse, yelping and bristling with fear. Running to find the cause of this commotion, they saw a huge tusked boar rise out of the brakes squinting at them, its hot breath snorting and panting on the morning air. The hide of the beast gleamed strangely white in a shaft of misty sunlight falling through the trees.

Immediately Pryderi called up his hounds again. Heartened by his shouts, the pack roused the boar where it grunted and steamed among the ferns. It stood at bay, bristling, with lowered tusks, giving only a yard or two of ground when Pryderi urged on the pack. As men and hounds closed in, the boar withdrew further into the wood, turned again, held its ground for a time with brief aggressive lunges of its white bulk that set the nervous hounds whimpering back on their heels; then it turned again and pulled back deeper still among the trees before making another stand. In this way Pryderi and Manawydan were drawn at last towards the far fringes of the copse. When they looked up they saw a tall fortress looming through the morning's sunlit haze. At that moment the boar made a last sally at the dogs and with a staggering turn of speed rushed over the outer mound of the fortress, across the ditch and up through the gate with the pack in hot chase after it.

Frowning at such queer behaviour Manawydan turned to his friend and asked who the hall belonged to.

'I thought I knew these lands better than my own hand,' said Pryderi. 'I have hunted all over them on horseback and on foot more times than I can remember, but I swear I have never come across this place before.'

'And have you ever seen a boar behave so oddly?'

'Never.'

'Then this is altogether a strange wonder,' Manawydan said. By this time they were standing on the outer mound of the castle and Pryderi would have gone further but Manawydan checked his friend's advance, saying that the strange behaviour of a white boar in a place they had never seen before smacked of enchantment and was not lightly to be trusted. So they stood for a time, watching for the hounds' return, listening for any cry, but an unnatural stillness hovered everywhere, as if the whole world was holding its breath.

At last Pryderi lost patience.

'If the hounds will not come out of their own accord,' he said, 'then we must go in and fetch them.'

'Not wise,' said Manawydan. 'I begin to think that this place was put here by whoever worked the first enchantment against us.'

'Why would they want to do more against us than they have already done?' Pryderi demanded. 'What offence have we given to any man?'

Manawydan shook his head in perplexity. 'Yet the power used against us has already left our condition grave. It would be foolish to put ourselves further at risk.'

'And cowardly to take flight!'

'Your wife and mine are waiting for us,' Manawydan reminded him.

'Then only one of us shall go, while the other waits to bring news if ...' – Pryderi hesitated a moment before completing the sentence – 'if I do not return. Being the stronger,' he added quickly, 'I am the one to go.'

'The strength of the body may not be enough,' Manawydan said. 'Who knows what is waiting for you in there, or who is working this magic against us?'

'Whoever it is,' Pryderi retorted, 'they shall not keep my hounds.' Then despite his friend's further protests he said, 'If I do not come back watch over my wife and mother for me, old friend,' and passed on over the ditch and up through the open gate.

When he found no sign of either boar or hounds in the empty courtyard, Pryderi advanced into the hall. That place too was entirely empty except that at the centre of the floor where he would have expected to find the hearth, there stood instead a drinking fountain raised on a marble slab. A gold cup was attached to the fountain's bowl by chains. The sound of water falling into cool marble left Pryderi's throat feeling still thirstier from the chase, so he crossed the hall, mounted the slab, and took the cup in his hands. Immediately he was frozen there, his hands glued to the gold cup, his feet fixed immobile to the marble slab. When he opened his mouth to shout no sound came out of it.

With increasing anxiety, Manawydan waited throughout the long day. By late afternoon, with the light already failing, he knew that his friend would not return, so he set off back through the wood with his dreadful news. Cigva broke down when she heard of Pryderi's disappearance. Holding the shaking woman in her arms, Rhiannon turned in desperate, angry accusation on her own husband, asking why he had abandoned her son.

Manawydan could only protest that he had counselled Pryderi against his rash action but there had been no stopping him.

Distraught himself, he demanded whether his wife would have preferred it if neither of them had returned.

'You might both be here now,' she said, 'if you had lent your strength to the adventure. A braver comrade would have done so.'

In their misery they wrangled for a time until Rhiannon declared at last that she would go to the accursed place herself and try to rescue Pryderi. Nothing that Manawydan could say would deter the impassioned woman, nor would she allow him to return to the fortress in her place. So he told Rhiannon how to find the way there, and took Cigva under his own protection greatly fearing that neither of them would see wife or husband again.

Rhiannon came safely through the wood to the fortress, entered by the still open gate, and saw her son standing alone and motionless at the fountain in the centre of the hall.

Exclaiming with relief, she ran across to him, asking why he had remained there that way, frightening them all so. Then she saw that her son could neither turn nor answer. Immediately she stepped onto the slab to pull him free, but as soon as her hands touched the golden cup she too was frozen there.

In the same instant lightning cracked across the night outside, thunder rolled, and as though it were no more than dust blown away by that sudden elemental violence, the fortress vanished with Pryderi and Rhiannon still captive inside it.

When dawn broke after a sleepless night Manawydan went back to the castle, saw that it was gone and knew that his fears of enchantment were confirmed.

Overwhelmed by the disaster that had overtaken her, and

seeing Manawydan return alone, Cigva told him she preferred death to life without her husband and Rhiannon. She could take no comfort in her wretchedness, so for a long time Manawydan could do no more than hold her, fighting his own grief and despair, until he felt the force of her weeping abate a little from its own exhaustion. Then he spoke softly to her, encouraging her to share his hope that Pryderi and Rhiannon were not dead but subject to some powerful enchantment. If it were to be lifted, it could only be through their own efforts, he said, and Cigva must therefore commit her strength, as he himself was doing, to finding ways by which they could be reunited with those they loved.

Having no other hope, Cigva took heart at his words and asked what they must do. The castle had vanished, Manawydan told her, their hounds were gone, and they could no longer make a living in Dyfed. They must go back into the world and wait on destiny there.

So they returned to the place where Manawydan had worked as a shoemaker and resumed their friendship with the goldsmith who made buckles for them. Gradually they began to prosper again until, once more, the rival cobblers threatened them with violence. But by then Manawydan had conceived a magical means to smoke out their enemies.

With the money he had made he bought enough seedcorn for three crofts of wheat, and sowed it as soon as he and Cigva returned to the hall at Arberth. The corn sprouted abundantly in all three crofts, and one afternoon came harvest time when Manawydan saw it standing tall and golden in his fields.

The next day he came out at dawn to reap the first field and found that all the ripened ears were gone and nothing left but the bare, broken stems. Cigva was disheartened at this further blow, and still more deeply so when Manawydan went out to reap the second field at first light on the next day only to find it too stripped bare. 'But having come twice,' Manawydan said patiently, 'the thief is sure to come a third time. I will keep watch over the last croft tonight.'

Arming himself, he took cover in the dark by the ripened wheat and at midnight heard a rustling like that of a breeze stirring among the corn. Getting to his feet he saw a swarm of mice moving through the crop like a grey mist. In their thousands they clambered up the stems, bent them under their weight, and gnawed off the ears in their tiny voracious jaws. Immediately Manawydan rushed among them, casting about till he saw one fatter and less nimble than the rest that was too slow to escape his grasp. Holding the mouse by the tail, he slipped it inside his glove, put the glove in his pocket and returned to where Cigva waited for him in the hall. When he hung his glove from a peg, Cigva asked him what was inside it.

'A thief,' he said, 'and one which I shall hang tomorrow.'

'What kind of thief could fit inside a glove?' she asked. So Manawydan told her of the swarm of mice and how he had managed to catch just one of them. 'But one may be enough,' he said, 'and the mouse shall hang on the morrow.'

'Is it not shameful,' Cigva answered 'for a man to torment so small a creature as a mouse?'

'Think so if you will,' said Manawydan, 'but the mouse shall be hanged nevertheless, and at my hand.'

'Then I must trust to your own good judgement,' said Cigva. And at dawn the next day Manawydan went to the enchanted mound where all their misfortunes had begun and planted two forked pieces of wood close together at its highest point.

He had just raised the second fork when he looked up and saw a man wearing a novice's robes approaching him. Manawydan greeted the stranger and asked where he had come from.

The novice said that he was travelling home from Lloegyr where he had been song-making in the cities there.

'This is very strange,' said Manawydan.

'Why so, friend?'

'Because yours is the first face I have seen in these parts for seven years,' said Manawydan, 'save only those of the friends I love.'

'What are you building there?' the novice asked.

'A gallows,' Manawydan answered.

'Who would you hang, friend?'

'A thief.'

'What manner of thief?'

When Manawydan held up the mouse by the tail, the novice said, 'Is it not degrading to one of your rank to be seen at such work? Let the mouse go, I pray you.'

'This mouse has robbed me and shall hang for it,' said Manawydan.

'A cruel way for a creature to die,' said the novice. 'I have a coin about me. Release the mouse in return for it.'

But Manawydan would not let the mouse go, so the novice shrugged, saying that the mouse could die for all he cared, and went on his way.

Then, as Manawydan was laying the cross-piece on the gallows, he saw a druid approaching him. Again he was engaged in conversation about the gallows and again met with protests when it was learned that he planned to hang a mouse. A larger sum of money was offered for a permanent stay of execution, but again Manawydan refused.

'Then let the creature hang,' said the druid and passed on his way.

So Manawydan slipped the noose about the neck of the mouse and was about to draw it up the gallows when he saw a large company approaching him with a man in all the robes and regalia of an archdruid at its head.

'What do you intend to do with that poor creature?' the archdruid demanded.

'As you can see,' said Manawydan, 'I'm about to hang it from this gallows I have built. The mouse is a thief who has robbed me. It deserves to die and if you will let me go about my work it shall shortly do so.'

'Stay your hand, friend,' said the archdruid. 'The sight of suffering is painful to my eyes. I have a great deal of money with me. Let me redeem the life of the mouse.'

'Not for all the gold in your wallet,' said Manawydan.

'And if I were to offer in addition to that all the horses and baggage in my train?'

'It would still not be enough to save this mouse from my just vengeance,' Manawydan declared firmly, turning back to his gallows again.

'Then name what price you will,' said the archdruid.

Manawydan paused in his work and stared at the white-faced man for a long moment.

'My price,' he said at last, 'is that Rhiannon and Pryderi be set free.'

'It shall be done,' said the archdruid.

Nodding and smiling, Manawydan said, 'But that is not all my price.'

'What else do you ask?'

'That the enchantment hanging over all the seven cantrefs of Dyfed be lifted.'

'That too shall be done,' the archdruid agreed. 'Now release the mouse.'

'Not yet,' said Manawydan. 'Not till I know who might be concealed beneath the shape of this mouse.'

'It is my wife,' said the archdruid.

'Your wife?' said Mamawyddan. 'And who might you be?'

'My name is Llwyd son of Cil Coed.'

'And if you can lift the enchantment on Dyfed then it was you that laid it there,' said Manawydan. 'I'm wondering why you would have done so foul a thing?'

'For my own just vengeance,' said Llwyd. 'I am kin to Gwawl son of Clud, who was gravely wronged by Pwyll when the Head of Annwn played "badger in the bag" with him.'

'Did not Gwawl forswear vengeance?' Manawydan frowned.

'He did, but his kin did not forswear it. I vowed to take vengeance on his behalf and I waited long to take it. It was I who put Dyfed under enchantment and drew Pryderi and Rhiannon into my power. It was my people who came as mice to take your harvest, Manawydan, and my ill fortune that you took my wife captive there. Nor would you have done that had she not been hampered by her pregnant belly. But since you have her, for her sake I shall do as you ask. Now will you set her free?'

Still Manawydan shook his head. 'Not unless you swear that you and your kin renounce all vengeance for this,' he said. 'And not only shall I be free of your retribution, Llywd son of Cil Coed, but so shall my wife Rhiannon, and Cigva and my friend Pryderi also.'

Llwyd nodded wryly at that. 'You have my oath on it then, and were wise to think of it, for be sure you would not have been free of great afflictions else. Now let that be an end of it. Give me back my wife.'

'Then your wife would be at your side and I no closer to mine,' said Manawydan. 'I will see Pryderi and Rhiannon first.'

'Look where they come then,' said Llwyd. He made a flourish of his arm, there was a sudden alteration in the light as though its insubstantial fabric was swiftly unfolding on itself, and in the same instant Manawydan saw Pryderi and Rhiannon standing on the mound beside him.

Smiling, Rhiannon said, 'I think in my distress I did you great injustice, husband.'

'And by ignoring your advice I brought greater troubles on us, friend,' said Pryderi.

'Yet are the ways of this world mysterious,' Manawydan smiled, 'and things must complete themselves as best they can.'

'What of my wife, old magician?' demanded Llyd. 'The enchantment on Dyfed will not lift until I have her.'

'Then is she yours again,' said Manawydan and lifted the noose from around the mouse's neck.

At that moment the mouse was transformed into a young pregnant woman of great beauty who hastened down the mound to rejoin Llwyd. As soon as she was beside him the whole company disappeared, leaving Rhiannon, Pryderi and Manawydan alone on the mound.

When they looked about them they saw Cigva running towards them from the hall at Arberth, and the hall itself was restored to its splendour, bright with life again. Smoke was rising from the hearth, the sound of distant feasting drifted faintly over the air, and across the abundant pastures of Dyfed the herds and flocks were grazing quietly at peace.

9

The Return of Lleu

In the days when Pryderi was King of Dyfed a powerful magician called Math son of Mathonwy ruled over the more northerly realm of Gwynedd. Math held his throne under a sacred restriction that required him to sit with his foot held in a virgin's lap at all times save those when he must lead his host in battle. His foot-bearer at the time of this story was Goewin daughter of Pebin, whose limpid beauty was renowned throughout the kingdom. The times were peaceful, so Goewin's ritual office kept her permanently at Math's side, and such constant intimacy led to the growth of a deep mutual affection between the priestess and her king.

Math governed Gwynedd from his seat at Caer Dathyl but because his movements were restricted, it was necessary for others to make the regular circuit of the kingdom for him. He entrusted this duty to the sons of his sister Don, two vigorous young men whose names were Gilfaethwy and Gwydion. The brothers acted faithfully enough on Math's behalf but whenever they came back to court Gilfaethwy found his eyes irresistibly drawn by Goewin's beauty. His dreams were filled with images of her face, he woke whispering her name. Soon he could think of little else until he was so powerfully consumed by fantasies of possessing her that the ungovernable desire began to affect his health and appearance. His moods grew ever more fractious and listless, there were hungry shadows round his eyes.

It wasn't long before Gwydion noticed the change in his brother. One day he asked what was troubling him.

'Why do you ask?' Gilfaethwy answered guardedly.

'Because the colour has gone from your face and the heart from your life,' said Gwydion, 'I am the brother who loves you and would share your troubles as I share your joys. Come now, tell me what ails you.'

'Nothing that talk will help,' said Gilfaethwy.

'And why is that?' asked Gwydion.

Gilfaethwy shook his dejected head. 'You know as well as I do that if anything is so much as whispered between two men it won't be long before wind of it reaches Math's ears.'

'So it's as I thought,' said Gwydion.

'What do you mean?'

'Your sighs grow heavier every time we leave the king. Much as we love him, it cannot be Math your heart is aching for, so it must be Goewin. Am I not right? You're sick with desire for Math's fair foot-bearer.'

'Is it so obvious?' said Gilfaethwy, aghast.

'I'm your mother's son,' said Gwydion. 'I'm closer to you than Goewin is to Math. I know your heart, brother, and I feel for it.'

'Then you know this pain will be the death of it.'

'Men die of hunger and may be killed by hate, but dying for love is a rarer thing. It's better to *live* for it, I think.'

'I do. It's all I think about.'

'Yes, brother,' said Gwydion, 'but what are you going to *do* about it?'

'What can I do? The thing's impossible.'

'Then put her from your mind.'

'Do you think I wouldn't if I could? I've tried. I swear I've tried. But she's always there, the thought of her, night and day. She's part of me, inside me, everywhere I turn.' Gilfaethwy turned his despairing, voracious gaze on his brother as if Gwydion were the only source of solace in an otherwise bitter and pointless world. 'I have to have her.'

'Then take her,' Gwydion said.

'If only it was that easy!'

'If a man really wants something,' said Gwydion with a wry conspiratorial smile, 'no one can stop him getting it. Especially if he has a brother who loves him.'

Gilfaethwy glanced up, a sudden fugitive glint of hope in his eyes. Then he shook his head and snorted. 'Apart from anything else,' he said, 'she never leaves Math's sight.'

'Except in time of war,' Gwydion reminded him.

'Unfortunately,' his brother sighed, 'we're not at war.'

'Not yet,' Gwydion said. 'But about that at least, something might be done.'

That night Gwydion presented himself before Math saying that during his recent circuit he had heard that an interesting new breed of animal had appeared in the south.

'What kind of animal might that be?' asked Math.

'The beasts are small,' said Gwydion, 'smaller than cattle, but their flesh is much sweeter and I hear their name changes. Sometimes they are called "pigs" and sometimes "swine".'

'Who owns these animals?' asked the king.

'Pryderi son of Pwyll the Head of Annwn. I understand that the pigs were sent as a gift out of Annwn by Arawn who was king there and friend to Pwyll.'

'So there are pigs in Annwn, and swine in Dyfed,' said Math, 'but neither in Gwynedd?'

'A situation to be remedied,' Gwydion agreed.

'And how would a man do that?'

'He might go to Arberth disguised as one of a company of bards and entertain Pryderi so royally with his stories that he felt able to ask for some of the swine in return.'

'And it is well known that there is no better storyteller than Gwydion son of Don,' said Math.

Gwydion nodded, smiling.

'And if Pwyll will not give you the pigs?' said Math.

Gwydion smiled again. 'Then I have other plans,' he said.

So taking ten men with them, Gwydion and Gilfaethwy headed south until they came to Ceredigiawn where Pryderi was keeping court. At the feast that night Gwydion enthralled the whole company with his stories, making them laugh and weep and gasp by turns, and taking their imaginations to such enchanted places that no one wanted to sleep. It was already far into the night when Pryderi said that the bard must at last be allowed to rest. Then he called Gwydion to his side and congratulated him on his silver tongue.

'May I use that instrument on my own behalf?' asked Gwydion.

'You have earned rich reward, friend,' Pryderi smiled. 'What gift had you in mind?'

'It would greatly please my own king,' said Gwydion, 'if I were to bring back some of the fine herd of pigs that were brought to

Dyfed out of Annwn.' He was looking Pryderi in the eye as he asked and saw his expression swiftly change.

'After tonight's entertainment I would gladly give you them,' Pryderi answered, 'but I've undertaken neither to sell any of the herd nor give them away until they have bred twice their own number, and that will not be for some time.'

Gwydion allowed an expression of dubious, judgmental disappointment to cross his face. Pryderi saw and was embarrassed by it. 'It pains me to refuse you, friend,' he said.

Gwydion nodded thoughtfully. 'Then if you will neither give me the swine nor refuse them to me tonight,' he suggested, 'perhaps tomorrow we can find another way.'

'If you can do that,' said Pryderi, 'then I will certainly think again.'

So withdrawing with his men, Gwydion told them he had failed to win the pigs directly and they must now resort to magical means. Using his powers of enchantment he created a team of twelve illusory stallions each saddled and bridled in what appeared to be the finest gold. Then he conjured twelve greyhounds harnessed to match them. The glossy pelt of each beast shone midnight-black above a flashing white underbelly, and as they all glistened with apparent vigour and health no finer spectacle had been seen in Dyfed for some time. Yet Gwydion was still not satisfied. Further exercising his art he transformed twelve toadstools into as many golden shields, and the next morning he presented the whole superb ensemble at court to excite Pryderi's admiration and desire.

'Having pondered the matter we spoke of last night,' Gwydion said, 'it occurs to me that though you have agreed neither to sell the swine nor to give them away as gifts, you have made no promise not to exchange them, which is surely the fairest mode of commerce between friends?'

'That is true,' said Pryderi.

'Then as I see you have a great admiration for these stallions and greyhounds and shields,' Gwydion went on, 'I would be happy to consider parting with them in exchange for the pigs.'

Thinking this too good a chance to miss, Pryderi said he would take counsel on the matter and found that his kinsmen felt the same way. So the exchange was promptly made, and after a joyful exchange of mutual thanks, Pryderi watched Gwydion and his friends drive away their herd of pigs, then turned back with delight to rejoice in his own splendid new acquisitions.

Meanwhile Gwydion told the others to make the best speed they could because the power of his spell would last only until the next day and then Pryderi and his host would be after them.

So they drove the pigs rapidly across country making for a settlement on the uplands of Gwynedd where they built a sty for the herd before returning to Caer Dathyl.

When they arrived back at court they found the whole place alive with the mustering of troops.

'Pryderi has called out all his twenty-one cantrefs against us,' said Math, 'and I see you don't even have the pigs you promised me.'

Gwydion told him to rest assured that the herd was hidden in a safe place. 'Then they'd better be worth fighting for,' Math answered and, relieving his foot-bearer of her sacred duty, he rode out at the head of his host to take up a position against the invading forces of Dyfed.

That night Gwydion and Gilfaethwy stole out of the camp under cover of darkness and came back to Caer Dathyl.

Making their way straight to the place where Goewin slept in Math's own chamber, Gwydion drove out all the attendants and held them at bay, while his brother climbed into Goewin's bed. Once there, Gilfaethwy found to his dismay and frustration that his secret passion was not shared. So silencing the virgin's frightened screams of protest, he unbuckled himself and took Goewin against her will.

The next day the host of Gwynedd met the men of Dyfed in murderous battle. Math's forces had the advantage of the higher ground and after a time Pryderi was forced to withdraw his men from the slaughter. Heartened by the retreat, Math pushed his host after them; but then Pryderi's troops regrouped, made a stand on more favourable ground, and the slaughter got worse. The fighting went on throughout the day until both sides were so badly mauled that Math decided to accept Pryderi's offer of a truce.

'This quarrel is between Gwydion and myself,' Pryderi shouted across the lines. 'There is no need for any further death among the men of Gwynedd and Dyfed if he dares to answer in single combat for the wrong he has done me.'

When Math turned to his nephew, Gwydion said he was ready enough to fight. So the deceiver and the deceived advanced between the lines and fell on one another. But Gwydion had magic among his weapons, and it was in that uneven struggle that Pryderi met his end.

The noble Prince of Dyfed was buried at Maen Tyriawg above the battlefield. Mourning him bitterly, the men of his host made their way back south again. Meanwhile, with the victory won, Math despatched Gwydion and Gilfaethwy on their circuit of the kingdom, and led the remainder of his host back to Caer Dathyl.

On his return that night, Math called for his foot-bearer to come to his chamber. With lowered head Goewin presented herself before him and said, 'You must find a virgin to hold your foot in her lap, lord.'

'What do you mean?' Math protested. 'I will have no other foot-bearer but you.'

'I am no longer fit to do it,' Goewin said. 'I am a woman now.'

Astonished Math demanded to know how this could possibly be, and Goewin told him how his sister's sons had broken into that very chamber while Math was with his army, and how Gwydion had guarded the door while Gilfaethwy raped her.

Filled with tender compassion for Goewin's distress, and with bitter fury at his nephews' treachery, Math vowed that redress would be found. He took the weeping woman in his arms, declaring that as she could no longer be his foot-bearer he would make her his wife and give her authority over his realm. Then across all Gwynedd a ban was put out on the sons of Don that no one was to give them food or drink or shelter.

Weeks went by in which Gwydion and Gilfaethwy lived a hunted outlaw life, constantly moving from one makeshift woodland refuge to another. At last, hungry and wretched, with nowhere left to turn, they were driven to throw themselves back on the king's mercy.

'The death of Pryderi together with many brave men, the violation of my priestess, and the dishonour you have brought on my own name – for all this I would gladly give you death,' said Math, 'were you not my sister's sons. But as it was by magic that you worked your evil, so by magic shall you atone for it; and as you have behaved like animals so shall you live like them.' Then he struck Gilfaethwy with his wand and transformed him instantly into a hind; and before Gwydion could escape, he too was touched by the wand and turned into a stag. 'Come here again in a year,' said Math, 'and bring your spawn with you.'

Exactly a year later a great barking of dogs was heard at the wall, and a stag and a hind were seen there with a sturdy fawn between them. Math took the fawn and transformed it into a boy called Hidden whom he kept beside him; but when he touched the hind with his wand again it was transformed into a wild boar, and the stag was turned into a sow. They too were driven off to spend a

year in the wilderness. The young boar they brought back with
them at the end of that time became a boy called Hychdwn. Then
the shape of a wolf and she-wolf were put upon Gwydion and
Gilfaethwy, and the wolf cub that was born of that last coupling
was named Bleiddwn.

'The three sons of the false Gilfaethwy shall be true champions,' Math prophesied at the end of the third year; and declaring
that this triple humiliation had been punishment enough, he
restored the brothers to their true shape and offered them his
friendship again.

It wasn't long before Gwydion set about working his way back into
the king's confidence, and when the question of appointing a new
foot-bearer was raised, he was ready with a suggestion.

'Who could be more fitting than your niece, Arianrod, daughter of Don?' he said.

'My niece and your sister,' said Math suspiciously.

'Than whom there is no fairer virgin in Gwynedd,' said Gwydion.

'So I hear,' said Math, 'if words are to be trusted. Bring your
sister to court and we will see for ourselves.'

So Arianrod was brought to Caer Dathyl and presented before
the king where Gwydion did all he could to make sure that his
sister made a favourable impression.

'You are fair enough to grace our court, and seem an eloquent
companion,' said Math, 'but are you a virgin still?'

'I have no other knowledge but that I am,' said Arianrod.

'A complicated answer,' said Math, 'but I have means to
increase your knowledge.'

Then he reached for his wand and leaning forward a little, held it out before Arianrod at knee-height. 'Step over this,' he smiled, 'and we will learn the truth of it.'

Having no choice in the matter, Arianrod stepped over the wand and immediately gave birth to a strong boy-child with flowing yellow hair. Crying out at the shock of it, Arianrod fled from the room hurriedly followed by Gwydion, who saw something else drop from her as she ran. Picking it up, he wrapped the caul in a scarf and hid it inside a chest before returning to face the king.

Math was greatly taken by the lovely child with the flowing hair, at once naming him Dylan; but no sooner was the word uttered than the infant made for the sea after which he had been named and took to that element as fluently as any fish. In all his days no wave ever broke beneath him, and for that reason he was called Dylan Eil Ton, the Son of the Wave. Even the sea itself wept when he was finally killed with a spear, and ever afterwards that was called one of the Three Unhappy Blows.

Some time after his sister's humiliation, Gwydion was woken by a noise coming from the chest in his chamber. Opening the lid he saw another infant boy unwrapping himself from the scarf. Gwydion picked up the child, stared at it smiling for a time, then took it to where a wet-nurse lived and asked her to raise the child for him.

The boy grew so quickly that by the time he was two he stood as tall as a four-year-old and was able to walk unaccompanied to the court. When he saw how sturdy and fair the boy was, and that a kind of brightness shone about him, Gwydion's love for him grew stronger still. Watching over him carefully till he was a four-year-old tall enough to be twice that age, Gwydion decided that the time had come to take the boy to meet his mother.

As soon as they arrived at Caer Arianrod, Gwydion's sister asked who the fair boy was.

'This is our son, sister,' said Gwydion, smiling.

Arianrod stared at the child in horror, appalled that her brother should have preserved this living evidence of her shame; but when she released the full tempestuous force of her fury on him, Gwydion calmly insisted that he thought it no shame to be parent to such a fine child.

'What is his name?' Arianrod demanded.

'He doesn't yet have a name,' said Gwydion.

'Then I swear it as a destiny on him that he shall have no name unless I grant it,' said Arianrod, 'which I shall never willingly do.'

'If you yourself no longer bear the name of maiden,' Gwydion answered angrily, 'the boy is not to blame for that. One way or another, I'll see to it that you give him a name whether you will it or not.'

Then he took the boy away and brought him to the seashore where Gwydion gathered dulse and sea-girdle and used his magical powers to transform part of the weed into the finest leather, while from the rest he conjured a fully-rigged boat with a sail. Putting the boy into the boat and pushing it out on the tide, Gwydion sailed along the coast to the cove beneath Caer Arianrod, beached the boat and sat on the strand with the boy, stitching the leather into shoes.

As soon as he saw that they had been spotted from the high caer, Gwydion used his magic to change their appearances, though the aura of brightness still shone about the boy; then he returned to his work, whistling, and waited to be questioned about his business there.

Hearing that there was a shoemaker working in fine leather on the beach, Arianrod sent down the measurements of her foot and ordered a pair. Gwydion deliberately made the shoes too large, but Arianrod was attracted by their design, agreed to pay for them and asked her messenger to bring back another pair the right size. This time Gwydion made the shoes too small so Arianrod was at last drawn down to the cove herself, marvelling that so gifted a shoe-maker couldn't fashion a pair to fit her.

'I needed to see your delicate foot for myself,' said Gwydion, drawing a new pattern in his leather.

While he was working a wren fluttered about their heads and perched on the mast of the boat. Stealthily drawing his little bow, the boy took swift aim and pierced the bird with an arrow between the sinew of its leg and the bone.

'Truly the bright one has a steady hand!' Arianrod cried, applauding the shot. 'What is his name?'

'He had none till you spoke,' said Gwydion triumphantly as the boat shrivelled back into seaweed, 'but you have given him one despite yourself. He is Llew Llaw Gyffes, the Bright One with the Steady Hand, and a fair name it is.'

Seeing how she had been tricked, Arianrod cursed Gwydion for the deceit. 'But no good shall come to the child of it,' she said, 'for I lay a destiny on him that he shall never bear arms unless I give them to him.'

'And though it may take me many years I will see that you give him those arms whether you will it or not,' Gwydion shouted after her.

So he withdrew with the boy to Dinas Dinlleu where he taught him all the arts of horsemanship and watched him grow into a handsome, good-natured youth, shining with the light of life and eager to take his place in the world of men.

One day Llew came to Gwydion asking if the time had not yet come when he too should be allowed to take arms like the warriors he saw around him.

'It is time indeed,' Gwydion answered, 'and tomorrow we shall go to the place where you will win them.'

As they approached Caer Arianrod together, Gwydion used his magic to change their shapes once more, then told the gatekeeper to send word that there were bards bringing entertainment for the court's delight. Immediately they were called to join the feast in the hall, where Gwydion kept Arianrod enthralled with his witty conversation and his powers of storytelling.

Though the hour was late when the company finally retired to bed, Gwydion was up before cockcrow working his enchantments. Then, at first light, the whole castle was thrown into turmoil by the clamour of alarm.

Arianrod rushed to the chamber where Gwydion had been lodged with Llew, beseeching their help. 'There are so many ships off the coast we can scarce see the water for them,' she cried. 'They are sending armed men ashore and there are not enough of us to fight off such a force unaided. Will you and your young friend bear arms on my behalf?'

'We are bards, lady,' said Gwydion, 'and carry no weapons of our own. But if there are arms here we will wield them for you gladly.' So Arianrod came back with two maidens bringing weapons and armour enough for both her guests.

'I can hear the host coming ashore,' Gwydion said. 'Quickly, lady – these maidens will help me arm while you arm the youth.'

'With all speed,' said Arianrod breathlessly and set about buckling the arms on the youth. When she had finished she asked Gwydion if she had done the job aright.

'Perfectly,' said Gwydion, 'and now we can take these weapons off again as we have no immediate use for them.'

'What do you mean?' Arianrod cried. 'Have you not seen the forces ranged against us?'

'There are no forces, lady,' said Gwydion smiling, 'except those mustered by my magic to frighten you into giving arms to our son. And see how willingly you did it, even though I once heard you vow to withhold them from him for ever.'

Astounded to find that her brother had duped her again, Arianrod's face whitened with rage. 'You may have tricked a name for the youth out of me, and fooled me into giving him arms, but no good shall come to your son from it, Gwydion. Nor will you deceive me into helping him again, for I put a destiny on him now that I can not undo.' She stared at Llew through narrowed eyes, then back at Gwydion. 'As long as he lives,' she said, 'he shall never have a wife that is born of any of the people now on earth.'

Aghast at the strength of this malediction, Gwydion shouted after his sister, 'Nevertheless a wife shall be found for him.' Then he left that place and took the youth back to Caer Dathyl where he consulted with Math about what might be done for the youth against his mother's curse.

Though Math had learned to mistrust Gwydion over the years he still preserved a secret admiration for the cunning man. He felt moreover that Lleu was one of the noblest young men he had ever seen and agreed that he was the victim of a great injustice. So the old magician put a charm of protection over Lleu's life that was so complex in its weave it rendered the young man virtually invulnerable.

Then Math combined the powers of his majesty with those of Gwydion and together they applied them to the problem of finding a wife for Lleu. As she could not be a woman born of human kind they decided to make a wife for him out of flowers. They gathered the blossoms of the oak, the broom and the meadowsweet, and working a spell of creation over them they conjured into being a graceful and delicate young woman whom they called Blodeuedd.

A great feast was held at Math's court for the marriage of Blodeuedd to Llew. By the end of it Gwydion had persuaded the king to give one of his most prosperous cantrefs in the uplands of Ardudwy as a wedding gift to the young couple

When the feast was over Lleu carried his bride away and established his court at Mur Castell. From there he governed his lands so wisely that it seemed all Arianrod's maledictions had been averted and he might live out his life in contentment.

A day came however when Lleu had to travel to Caer Dathyl, leaving Blodeuedd alone at Mur Castell.

Restless in her tedious solitude, she was stirring aimlessly about the court when she heard the sound of a hunting horn echoing across the valley. Her heart lifted with sudden excitement at the belling of a pack of hounds in full cry. Gathering her skirts, she hastened to the wall in time to see an exhausted stag foaming at the mouth as it loped across the flank of the hill in the ruddy afternoon light. Already exhausted, it was straining to stay ahead of the hounds while the huntsmen came up quickly after them, winding their horns, and a smaller party followed behind on foot. They were dashingly dressed, vivid with the elation of the chase, and seemed to bring all the glamour of the wide world into her empty afternoon.

At once Blodeuedd called out to one of the lads watching from the wall to go and find out who this company were. He returned a short time later with the news that the hunt was led by Gronw Pebyr, the Lord of Penllyn. Blodeuedd had never met the man but she had heard much of him and experienced a flash of irritation now that her husband was not there to invite him to stay at Mur Castell and enliven their dull life for a time.

Meanwhile she saw that the stag had strength enough left to reach the banks of the Cynfael river but before it could cross it would be pulled down by the frantic hounds. From her distant vantage point Blodeuedd watched the kill with flame in her throat, thrilled by the frenzy of the dogs and the wild elation of the huntsmen. By the time the stag had been flayed and quartered and the hounds baited on its flesh, the light was beginning to fail. Dusk closed over her like the undesired ending of a story that had enchanted her heart.

Watching the weary exultant hunters turn back up the hill, Blodeuedd found herself longing to join them. The longer she watched the more the yearning grew till she could not bear the imminent prospect of their disappearance in the gloom. So she told her attendants it would be thought ill if they left the hunters to make their way back to Penllyn through the dark, and an invitation was sent out to Gronw Pebyr offering the hospitality of Mur Castell that night.

The offer was swiftly and gratefully accepted. Blodeuedd herself welcomed the hunters at the gate and showed them where to cleanse themselves before dining with her in the hall.

In the meantime, left alone again she felt an agitation of the heart such as she had never known before, as though she were being pulled on a swift, dark tide towards some destination she already knew but dare not name.

Only when she and Gronw Pebr sat in conversation at the table, drawing each other deeper into one another's gaze, did she recognize that the life she had lived up to that moment had been none of her choosing. Happy as she had been with Llew, her marriage suddenly seemed mere acquiescence in what had been decided for her by others rather than a mutual celebration of desire. It was as if her soul had been asleep. But now she was awake, alive in every pore of her being; and what that life wanted was a quickening of the passion coursing through her veins. 'Friend,' she said to Gronw Pebyr, and 'Friend,' he answered; yet neither found the rich word rich enough to speak the difficult treason of their dream.

Long before the meal was over Blodeuedd knew she would not go to her bed alone that night.

When Gronw rose to leave at dawn she drew him back into the bed beside her, saying that it would be many hours before Lleu returned and there was no reason why they should not spend that time deepening the joy they had found together. Gronw had no desire to leave her embrace, nor would Blodeuedd have permitted it if he had tried, so the morning and the afternoon were passed urging each other to the limits of their sensuality in fierce and tender exploration of the passion between them. When no word came of Lleu's return they went into another night, utterly intoxicated with one another and swearing that neither of them could bear the thought of parting. By the next morning, when word came that Lleu would remain another night at Caer Dathyl, it seemed that destiny was conspiring with them.

That night they lay awake in the dark for a long time, naked in each other's embrace, grieving at the separation that must soon come, unable to accept it.

'After all that has chanced between us,' Blodeuedd said, 'I can never return to my life as it was.'

'Nor I,' Gronw answered, 'but your husband will return. He will be here with you tomorrow. He will want to bring you to this bed. And to think of that maddens my heart.'

'And mine,' Blodeuedd whispered. 'I want only you.'

'Then he must be faced with the truth of it. You must tell him that you are mine now and his marriage is at an end. Let him find another wife.'

'There can be no other wife for Lleu,' said Blodeuedd in despair. 'His mother's curse prevents it. He believes that I was made for him. He would kill me rather than lose me.'

For a time the lovers lay unmoving, as if tethered together inside their own silence as they listened to the shriek of an owl across the night outside. They felt their minds racing to the beat of their blood. Though not a word was exchanged between them they felt their thoughts converge.

'There is only one answer,' said Gronw at last.

'His death?' she whispered.

'Yes.'

'Do you have the heart for that?'

'I do. I will come to Mur Castell and offer combat for you.'

'Then you would lose both me and your own life,' Blodeuedd replied, shaking her beautiful delicate head. 'Math himself has protected Lleu's life with a powerful enchantment. There is only one way that he can be killed.'

'Do you know the secret of it?' asked Gronw.

'No one knows that secret except Lleu himself.'

Again there was a long silence until Gronw released his breath in a heavy sigh. Blodeuedd laid her slender arm across his chest but he lifted it away as if the weight was too much for him.

'Then it seems we must choose either to live apart or to die together,' he murmured bitterly.

'Unless ...'

'Yes?'

'Unless I can learn Lleu's secret from him.'

Again the silence.

'Do you think you can do that?' Gwydion whispered.

'I am his wife,' Blodeuedd said. 'Surely there should be no secrets between us!'

Then the two of them laughed together, uneasily but with a fierce, breathless exhilaration at the dreadful destiny that was unfolding between them now.

So Gronw Pebyr left for Penlynn that day and Lleu Llaw Gyffes rode home to Mur Castel in happy ignorance of how the world had changed. A feast of welcome was arranged for his return, at which Lleu ate well and drank well and regaled his wife with stories about the merry time he had spent at Caer Dathyl in the good company of Gwydion and Math. Then, pleasantly exhausted from his journey, he stretched and yawned and told Blodeuedd that he was ready for the pleasures of their bed.

But the wife who lay down beside him that night was strangely silent and unresponsive to his touch. Concerned to find his tender approaches so unusually rebuffed, Lleu asked Blodeuedd what was the matter. Had he angered her? Was she ill?

'None of those things,' she answered.

'Then what is it?' Lleu asked. 'Something is troubling you. How shall I know what it is unless you tell me.'

'There is a thought preying on my mind,' Blodeuedd said.

'What thought is that?'

'It is the thought of your death.'

Lleu laughed at that. 'I have no intention of dying,' he reassured her.

'Don't laugh at me,' she said unhappily, then turned urgently towards him. 'It was while you were away,' she said. 'I grew so lonely for you and only the thought of your return consoled me. Then I realised how terrible it would be if you did not return, if you were to die before me and I was left to live out the long waste of years alone.'

Smiling, Lleu gathered her up in his arms. 'Did ever wife love her husband so?' he said. 'But I am young and well and there are many years before us. And we shall spend those years together, happily in one another's arms like this. What need to darken your sweet mind with thoughts of death?'

'I am not a child, Lleu,' she reproached him, 'and I know the world for a violent and hazardous place. Even at the height of your vigour some man might slay you.'

Laughing, Lleu shook his head. 'Put your mind at rest,' he said. 'It is no easy thing to slay me unless the gods will it.'

'How do you know that?'

'Because of the protection that is on me. I can be killed only in such complicated and contradictory circumstances that the world would have to change before they could happen. I will die an old man in my bed. Till then you need not trouble your head with thoughts of death.'

'Are you sure of that?' Blodeuedd asked.

'Quite sure.'

Then she sighed as if content and snuggled closer to him. After a time Llew reached out his arm to embrace her again, she responded softly to his kiss, but then as he moved to lie over her she turned suddenly away.

'What is it?' he asked.

'My mind is not yet at peace,' she said.

'But why not? Have I not told you there is no need for this anxiety.'

'You have told me that the circumstances in which you can be killed are complicated and contradictory.'

'Yes?'

'Then if that is so, how will you remember what they are?'

'Because I have them firmly in my mind.'

'*Now* you do; but how if you should forget?'

'I will not forget.'

'Time passes and memory fades,' Blodeuedd said, 'especially when the demands on it are great. The affairs of the cantref fill your mind with new things every day, and you have to remember many of them from year to year. As you grow older and busier and more forgetful, may not such matters drive more important memories from your mind?'

Lleu sighed impatiently. 'That will not happen.'

'But should we not make sure of it?'

'*There is no need, I tell you.*'

'Why are you angry?' she said. 'I speak only out of care.'

Looking down into her injured eyes and seeing that the moment for lovemaking had somehow slipped past him, Lleu regretted his impatience and lay back sighing on the bed. 'I see we shall have no peace until your mind is at rest,' he said. 'What more can I say that will calm it?'

'I thought you would be touched by my care,' Blodeuedd said, turning away, 'but as you think me no more than a foolish woman there is nothing more to say.'

Faced now with the prospect of a long miserable silence between them, Lleu hastened to reassure his wife that he thought no such thing, that he loved her dearly and had always stood in awe of her wisdom in all things.

'Then why will you not attend to me now?'

'I will,' he said. 'I am. What do you want me to do?'

After a long moment Blodeuedd said, 'It would greatly calm my heart if you entrusted me with the secret of your protection.' And, before he could speak, she added, 'Your life is the one thing that matters to me, I have no other concerns, and I am sure therefore never to forget it, however complicated it is. As long as I know the secret we can keep your life safe from harm.'

Lleu looked into her eyes again and saw the tears glistening there. 'If I tell you,' he said, 'will you be at peace?'

'I will,' she whispered.

'Then know,' he said, 'that I can be killed only with a poisoned spear that has been a year in the making and worked on only during the time of the ritual sacrifice on the high holy days of that year.'

'That would be a hard thing to do,' said Blodeuedd.

'And even if such a sacred lance were to be made,' Lleu went on, 'I can be slain neither inside a house nor outside it, and neither on horseback nor on foot; nor is that the whole of my protection.'

'Even so,' said Blodeuedd, 'I cannot see how any of this could be done. Yet to put my mind at rest you must tell all. How can your death be accomplished?'

'In one way only,' said Lleu. 'A bath must be prepared for me by a riverbank and a thatched awning raised over the tub. Then if I were to stand with one foot on the edge of the bath and the other on the back of a he-goat that had been tethered there, I might be slain by a thrust of that sacred spear.' He smiled at her then. 'Now do you understand at last why you need have no anxiety.'

'I do,' Blodeuedd answered, coming closer to him, 'and I thank those who made me that they have put my husband under such good protection.'

The next day she sent word of what she had learned to her lover, Gronw Pebyr, Lord of Penlynn.

A year later word came back to her that the spear was made.

In bed that night Blodeuedd tossed and turned restlessly again until Lleu asked what was troubling her.

'You will be impatient with me,' she said; and when Lleu promised he would not, she confessed that she was worrying again about the manner in which he might be killed. 'I feel the need to fix those complicated circumstances in my mind more surely than words can do,' she said.

'How could that be done?' Lugh asked drowsily.

'Tomorrow when you take your bath,' she said, 'could we not place the tub by the river and raise the awning over it, and bring a he-goat there so that you can show me exactly what those circumstances are that we must avoid?' And then, before he could protest, she added, 'Surely such an improbable conjunction of events could happen only once in the history of time. By arranging them safely for ourselves we would prevent them from ever happening again.'

'Do you really have such anxious care for my life?' said Lleu in loving wonder.

'I do,' said Blodeuedd, 'and cannot sleep for the constant anxiety of it.'

'Then if it will ease your heart,' he said, 'I will do it.'

On the next day Blodeuedd ordered the servants to carry a great silver cauldron to the banks of the Cynfael and raise a thatched awning above it. When the shelter was built to her satisfaction she called Lleu to come and see her work.

'Now you must take your bath, lord,' she said, smiling.

'Gladly,' he said, took off his robe and climbed into the steaming water. She chatted with him there in the shade of the thatch for a time, soaping his back and arms, seeing them glisten in the morning light. The goat grazed innocently beside them, munching the grass in its yellow teeth and staring at the laughing man and woman every now and then through the black slots of its eyes. Then when Lleu was cleansed and rinsed, Blodeuedd said, 'The goat is by you, lord. Show me now the position in which you must never stand again.'

Shaking his drenched head and smiling at her, the naked man lithely lifted one foot to the rim of the bath, balanced there a moment with the water dripping from his skin, then brought his other bare foot down to rest on the back of the goat. His body glittered with vigour. Never had he felt so alive.

At that moment Gronw Pebyr rose up from the place where he had concealed himself, balanced the spear in his hand and sent it shining through the air.

The spear struck Lleu in the side and hung there quivering. He looked down at it with astonished eyes, then put both hands to the shaft in an effort to withdraw it. The very air was bright with pain. In a slow release of blood the shaft came out leaving the head behind. For an instant Lleu stared down in bewilderment where his wife stood before him, white-faced, one hand across her mouth, unable to withdraw her gaze from his. Then, in that endless moment when she expected her husband to topple at her feet, the figure of Lleu vanished inside the harsh morning glare. In his place she saw a sudden savage beating of black wings, a sharp glint of talons and beak. Uttering a shriek that tore the steamy air between bath and awning, a black eagle spread its great pinions above Blodeuedd's cowering head and disappeared into the sky.

Some time later word came to Caer Dathyl that Lleu Llaw Gyffes had vanished and was presumed dead. Later it was learned that Blodeuedd was now wedded to the Lord of Penlynn who was settled in Mur Castell and had subdued all the cantref around Ardudwy.

If the news brought grief to Math's heart, it left Gwydion utterly distraught. Swearing to Math that he would not rest until he had news of Lleu's fate, the magician set out in search of his lost son.

Eventually Gwydion's travels brought him to Maenar Penardd where he passed the night in a peasant's house. There he learned of the strange behaviour of the man's sow – a great moon-bellied animal with a grin like a snare that would burst from the sty every morning, stay out all day and not return till night, by which time the bristles at her snout were stained with blood.

'Where does she go?' asked Gwydion, and when he was told that the sow was gone too fast for any man to follow her, he decided to keep track of her movements himself the next day.

Gwydion tracked the sow upstream to a valley between Snowdon and the sea which is still called Nantlleu. There he found the animal beneath an oak gorging on a heap of rotten flesh that was crawling with maggots. Looking up into the tree, Gwydion saw a black eagle perched at the crown, and every time it preened itself or ruffled its feathers, more rotten flesh fell to the ground from the wound in its side.

Gwydion approached the oak more closely, stepping quietly so as not to startle the great bird, and lifted his voice in song:

An oak grows between two lakes,
Darkened are both sky and glen.
Shall I not know by this foul wound
That Lleu is here?

Hearing the strains of this verse, the eagle spread its wings and flew down to a lower bough as if to listen more closely. Encouraged, Gwydion sang again:

An oak grows on upland ground
Drenched by the rain of nine-score storms,
Yet does it not bear amongst its boughs
The pain of Llew Llaw Gyffes?

Once more the eagle spread its pinions to glide through the air till it gripped the oak's lowest bough. Again Gwydion sang:

An oak that grows beneath a mount,
Refuge of the darkened light.
If I speak truth shall it not be Lleu
That flies into my lap?

Then Gwydion knelt with one knee to the ground and the great grieving bird swooped out of the tree and came to roost at his thigh. Immediately Gwydion struck the eagle with his wand and Lleu resumed his own shape again; but he was haggard and thin, all strength drained from his wasted body by the poison of the spear, and so pitiful was the sight of him that Gwydion wept.

Gwydion carried Lleu back to Caer Dathyl where he and Math worked for his recovery employing the best skills of all their physicians. Before the year was out Lleu was restored to the full vigour of his strength again. One day he presented himself before Math saying that the time had come for him to seek redress for the grave injury that had been done to him.

Math nodded his assent. 'The Lord of Penlynn still holds court with Blodeuedd at Mur Castell,' he said, 'and while that lasts there can be no justice in the world.'

So Gwydion and Lleu mustered their forces and set out for Ardudwy. When Blodeuedd heard that her husband was alive and returning in search of vengeance her courage failed her. Abandoning Gronw Pebyr she fled into hiding with her women in the mountains across the Cynfael river. Abject at her defection, Gronw himself fled from Mur Castell to shelter in his own hall at Penlynn.

When he heard that Lleu was coming for him there, Gronw sent word offering whatever price in gold and land Lleu might name in atonement for the harm that had been done to him. But Lleu was implacable. The message was returned that only one price would satisfy the transfigured lord: he would have Gronw stand as he himself had once stood, at the bath under the awning, where all the impossible contraries converged, that Lleu might cast a spear at him.

Gronw trembled when this message was brought to him. Turning to his followers, he asked if any of them loved him enough to stand there in his stead and take the blow; but no man was prepared to die for his lord that way and for that reason Gronw's warband was known ever afterwards as one of the Three Disloyal Hosts.

So Gronw returned alone to Mur Castel and there by the Cynfael river he saw where the thatched awning stood with the silver cauldron beneath it and the male goat tethered beside.

Lleu was waiting for him there, his oiled body bright in the sunlight, with a lance balanced in his hand.

'For myself, lord,' Gronw entreated him, 'I intended you no harm. It was the woman's wiles that led me to do the evil I did.' And when Lleu gave him no answer he said, 'Because of that I beg you to let me place a stone between the place where I will stand and the place from which you cast your spear.'

Holding his gaze in his own steady eyes, Lleu nodded at him.

'Choose your stone,' he said.

So Gronw exerted all his strength to set up a stone in front of the thatched awning, and when he felt sure it would protect him from the blow he took up his position with one foot on the rim of the bath and the other resting on the goat's back.

Lleu lifted his spear and hurled it with such force that it penetrated the stone and passed on through to take Gronw in the midriff and break the spine in his back. That stone still stands on the banks of the Cynfael in Ardudwy and is known to this day as Gronw's stone.

So Lleu Llaw Gyffes came back into possession of his lands where he ruled prosperously for many years until eventually he became Lord of all Gwynedd.

As for Blodeuedd, she was found that night by Gwydion cowering among her women on the bare mountainside beyond the river. She went down on her knees imploring him not to kill her, and as Gwydion looked down on the beautiful, treacherous creature he had helped to conjure out of flowers, he shook his head and said, 'No, you shall have a more shameful fate than death. Because of the dishonour you brought on your husband you shall never show your face by day again.'

Then he took his wand and touched her with it, and in that moment she was transformed for ever into an owl, the bird that is most shunned by other birds and hates above all things else the exposing light of day.